CORPORATE CULTURE

CORPORATE CULTURE

ILLUMINATING THE BLACK HOLE

Jerome Want, Ed.D.

ST. MARTIN'S PRESS　NEW YORK

www.stmartins.com

Design by Maura Rosenthal/MSpace

Library of Congress Cataloging-in-Publication Data

Want, Jerome H.
    Corporate culture : illuminating the black hole / Jerome Want.—1st ed.
        p. cm.
    ISBN-13: 978-0-312-35484-8
    ISBN-10: 0-312-35484-3
    1. Corporate culture. I. title.

    HD58.7.W327 2007
    658.4'063—dc22

                                                                2006050617

First Edition: January 2007

10 9 8 7 6 5 4 3 2 1

This book is dedicated to the memory of Frances J. Burns,
a most astute observer of organization culture,

and to the countless workers who strive to improve
the corporate cultures of their own organizations.

CONTENTS

ACKNOWLEDGMENTS

No author writes a book by himself, and this author is no exception. I am most indebted to a number of people who have provided invaluable insight and feedback, as well as technical support, including: David Baldwin and Jeffrey Bleustein of Harley-Davidson Motor Company, Jim Coblin of Nucor Corp., Michael Lorelli of Latex International, Dr. Frank LaFasto of Cardinal Health Systems, Dr. David Marion of Berwyn, Pennsylvania, Barrie Novak of Cisco Systems, Jeneanne Rae of Peer Insight, Dr. Jeanette Shallop of Indianapolis, Indiana, Nancy Metivier and Robert Stiller of Green Mountain Coffee Roasters, Dr. David Ulrich of the University of Michigan, George Vojta of E Standards Forum, David Wickenden of Fleishman-Hillard, Scott Williams of Starwood Hotels, Kim Wissman of the Ohio Public Utility Commission, Amy Yasneski of the Phillips Corporation, and, most especially, Dr. Julian Stein and Carolyn Stein, who helped make this book possible. I also wish to thank Bill Harrison of the Harrison Group, of Vienna, Virginia, for his expert technical assistance in constructing the figures and charts that have contributed so much to the book. Ultimately, any opinions expressed in this book are mine alone.

A NOTE TO THE READER

In my first book, *Managing Radical Change: Beyond Survival in the New Business Age* (Wiley, 1995), my goal was to present a systematic "road map" or process for better understanding radical change as it affected the business world. I accomplished that goal through the presentation of the Business Change Cycle—an original and proven model for better understanding how change impacts business performance. It took change out of the realm of abstract discussion to one where business professionals, at all levels, could plan for and better manage radical change as it affected their own business organizations. Radical change (as opposed to incremental change) first became a major feature of the business landscape in the 1970s as traditional business planning and management practices had been rendered obsolete in a less predictable and more chaotic business environment. The pace of radical change has not diminished in the twenty-first century, with entire industries—not just major companies—succumbing to radically changed business conditions. The business world has responded with a host of silver bullets and all-purpose fads and fix-its that have done very little to help companies effectively manage change, much less utilize change to competitive advantage.

The heart of the problem, as well as the solution, rests within every company regardless of its size or past successes. It is called "corporate culture." I devoted one chapter of *Managing Radical Change* to the subject of business culture, knowing that it deserved a book unto itself. No corporate change effort can succeed while relying on underperforming, bureaucratic, and outdated business cultures. Scores of industry-leading companies have failed for a variety of reasons, such as poor planning, missed market opportunities, flawed acquisitions, failed or obsolete products, inadequate leadership, insufficient research and development, corporate malfeasance, or poor governance. The list goes on. *Rarely is a company's failure attributed to its failed culture and just as rarely is a successful company's culture credited for its achievements.* It is with that in mind that I have written this book. In effect, I am turning chapter five from *Managing Radical Change* inside out to provide an in-depth look at corporate culture within the context of a radically changing competitive environment. As with my first book, my approach remains nonacademic, examining culture in the business world within the context of real-world business events and change. Nevertheless, where necessary, I draw on the thoughts of leading academics to further support the reader's understanding. I present the subject in a manner that directly relates to day-to-day business practices within the corporate environment. I will also refer to the subject of culture in the government sector, but only to draw illustrative parallels where necessary. This book is about culture in the business world. I have employed another of my models—the Hierarchy of Business Cultures—around which this book is written. I have also revisited the Business Change Cycle with updates that my clients have found useful in recent years and which relate directly to the subject of this book.

I use, interchangeably, the terms "culture change" and "culture building" throughout the book. In most cases, they can be interchangeable; however, culture building can also be reserved for newer, emerging companies, and culture change can be directly linked to more established companies with mature and relatively unchanging cultures. I also frequently use the term "process" in the book. I dislike the term "program," which, in my mind, implies a predetermined, static set of actions that are unchanging and have a definite end point. *Proper culture building and change is a dynamic, ongoing process that is open to new directions and ideas and must be continued as long as the business organization exists.* If companies are to effectively manage the forces of radical change in support of improved corporate performance, they must recognize that their success will depend on their ability to replace outdated, ignored, and failed business cultures with entirely new performance-driven cultures that will also function responsibly and ethically.

I have several supporting objectives in writing this book.

First, help readers better understand the critical issue of culture and to demystify the subject.

Second, forge a direct link, in the reader's mind, between business performance and business culture.

Third, demonstrate that a company's ability to effectively manage the forces of radical change will depend directly upon its own internal culture.

Fourth, help business professionals, regardless of title, position, or area of responsibility, understand how they are affected by corporate culture and how they affect the culture around them.

Fifth, help identify and overcome barriers to effective culture building.

Sixth, provide insight into companies with high-performing business cultures and how the CEOs and employees in these companies perform.

Finally, provide a blueprint for the culture building process or what I call "operationalizing" corporate culture.

I must emphasize, however, that reading a book such as this one or others on the subject or convening discussion seminars within the company will not, by itself, turn the reader or the larger organization into culture change experts. That requires actively undertaking the culture change process itself.

Corporate culture is not one thing a CEO does—
it is everything he does.

—Louis Gerstner,
Chairman and Chief Executive Officer (ret.),
IBM

PART I CORPORATE CULTURE IN THE AGE OF RADICAL CHANGE

1

IT'S ABOUT CHANGE

Change has considerable psychological impact on the human
mind.
To the fearful, change is threatening because it means that things
may get worse.
To the hopeful, change is encouraging because things may get
better.
To the confident, change is inspiring because the challenge exists
to make things better.

—King Whitney Jr.

Few terms in the American business lexicon have been more ignored or
misunderstood than "corporate culture." With the unending stream of
corporate scandals, the spectacular failures of such blue-chip companies as Enron, WorldCom, Sunbeam, and Arthur Andersen, as well as
the implosion of many former hypergrowth companies, such as Lucent
Technologies, Cambridge Technology Partners, Krispy Kreme, Tyco,
Global Crossing, Cray Computer, and Compaq, corporate culture
is suddenly the focus of attention in the business media and is a topic
of discussion in corporate boardrooms. The term "corporate culture"
is now linked most often to cases where it has failed for reasons of
ethical wrongdoing, neglectful board oversight, or privileged and profligate senior management. Nevertheless, the impact of corporate culture transcends malfeasance on mahogany row. It contributes directly
to a company's ability—or inability—to effectively manage radically

changing competitive business conditions. Properly nurtured, corporate culture may be the last and only reliable resource for a company needing to deal with radical change.

Failed corporate cultures have contributed to the downfall of many companies, including the original AT&T, Adelphia, Hospital Corporation of America (HCA), Kmart, General Motors, Kodak, Polaroid, Tenet Healthcare, Qwest, Rite Aid, as well as Delta Air Lines and most of its legacy airline competitors. The list is not limited to the business world, for failed organization culture is apparent in a wide range of government, nongovernmental (NGO), and nonprofit organizations. Consider the nonstop criticisms of the Federal Bureau of Investigation since the 9/11 attack. FBI Director Robert Mueller has repeatedly attributed his agency's failures to its unchanging culture. The Federal Emergency Management Agency (FEMA) was harshly criticized for its failure to respond proactively to two natural disasters: Hurricane Katrina in 2005 and Hurricane Andrew in 1992. Incompetence and a frozen bureaucracy were seen as the causes.

The Immigration and Naturalization Service (INS), Central Intelligence Agency (CIA), National Aeronautics and Space Administration (NASA), Internal Revenue Service (IRS), and U.S. Postal Service have all been chastised for their waste and ineffective performance. In addition, many prominent nongovernmental agencies, such as the Red Cross, U.S. Olympic Committee, the United Way, and, of course, the United Nations, at times, have all been cited for their bureaucratic performance and outright corrupt cultures. *Failed culture is not just about wrongdoing at the top. It is about failed performance at all levels of the organization.* Widespread incompetence, ineffective communications and information sharing, inability to anticipate and plan for changes in the competitive environment, failure to promote open discussion and critical feedback, as well as lapsed enforcement of ethical standards, are several of many contributors to underperforming and failed cultures. In this book, we will focus our attention on culture in the world of business—high-performing cultures, failed cultures, and those in between.

OUTDATED CORPORATE CULTURES

From one perspective, it is refreshing to have the recent wave of business failures and CEO firings laid at the altar of failed business cultures. For too long, sound corporate culture building and management have been pushed aside in favor of failed, oversold, and overused magic bullets that have delivered little in the way of sustained business performance. Instead, companies should have been finding ways to rebuild, reinvent, and plan better business cultures in support of their business objectives. Companies such as AT&T, Arthur Andersen, Compaq, Digital Equipment, Bethlehem Steel, Adelphia, Cray Computer, SmithKline (and its three successor entities French, Beckman, and Beecham), Firestone, Enron, and Kmart, to name just a few, owe their failures to their overreliance on outdated and failed corporate cultures. "Performance-degrading cultures have a negative financial impact on companies and inhibit their ability to adopt needed strategic and tactical changes" (J. Kotter & J. Heskett, *Corporate Culture and Performance*, Free Press, 1992). American businesses, in particular, must begin to build corporate cultures that can adapt to very different market conditions as competition now comes from all over the globe with the ability to produce and deliver products and services to any country or economy.

Because a company was once an industry leader does not make it immune to the impact of radical change. Former industry-leading companies have lost critical market share, in part, because they ignored or mismanaged their cultures—companies like Xerox, Lucent, Hewlett-Packard, Rite Aid, Wang Laboratories, American Home Products (now Wyeth Aerst), Merck, SAP, Motorola, and Sears. Indeed, entire industries have failed as a result of their failed industrywide cultures, with the steel, airline, and home savings and loan industries topping the list. *When companies are not able to change their cultures, they cannot expect to be successful in responding to radically changing business conditions in the marketplace. They will fail.*

Radical change has become the only constant in today's business world, and no industry or company has been spared its impact. In my last book, *Managing Radical Change: Beyond Survival in the New Busi-*

ness Age (Wiley, 1995), I detailed deregulation and increased regulation, industry consolidation, divestitures, the technology explosion, and the globalization of product markets as the major forces for change. These forces continue to pose new challenges as well as to present opportunities for American corporations and industries in today's highly competitive environment. Nevertheless, the pace of change has become even more—not less—rapid, relentless, and unpredictable. While some corporate leaders look hopefully to a period of predictable and stable markets, radical change is here to stay. It is a permanent component of the competitive landscape.

Unfortunately, companies continue to rely on very conventional business practices and remedies to cope with the radically changing competitive conditions that threaten their very survival. *At the heart of the problem is that most American companies have done little to change their corporate cultures in response to a radically changed competitive environment.* All sorts of remedies, interventions, and "can't-fail fads and fix-its" have cost billions of dollars, while companies and industries continue to stumble and fail when confronted by radical change. *Only a few unique enterprises have begun to recognize that nothing less than a total rethinking and transformation of their corporate cultures will be required to turn change into a competitive advantage, not a liability.*

THE SHOCK OF RADICAL CHANGE

Between World War II and the early 1980s, most companies found ways to stay in business in what was then a relatively stable market environment. Incremental growth or just holding on to existing market share was enough to keep many marginal companies in business. Both the structure and cultures of virtually every American business were based on a rigid and hierarchical command-and-control management model. People at the top did all the planning and expected those below to implement those plans without question or deviation. A successful workforce strictly obeyed orders from above, kept costs down, and continually improved productivity. Worker feedback was rare, and larger issues of culture performance, organization, and management effectiveness simply did not exist. This reflected the long-outdated Taylor school of management at work.

The Taylor model had been the essence of Western-style business management since the midnineteenth century. It was based on a highly quantitative and authoritarian engineering model, developed by Charles Taylor, in which people were little more than interchangeable parts in a larger production process. Corporate culture was never an issue. The Taylor model may have been appropriate for wartime production and the efficient deployment of a global military force, but it has many failings in today's business climate. Its defects remained hidden for nearly twenty years after World War II as American business was largely unchallenged around the globe. Not until Japan and Germany rebuilt their economies were American companies challenged. German businesses emphasized the importance of labor to the company and welcomed the creation of unions. Japanese businesses were rebuilt through the power of consensus and a commitment to lifetime employment for employees in their companies. Both were reactions to the authoritarian regimes that had ruled those countries prior to and during World War II.

Eventually, German and Japanese companies were seen as threats to American business dominance, and there were loud cries for American companies to start to emulate Japanese management practices, including the keiretsu—the interlocking businesses that would probably be deemed in violation of U.S. antitrust laws. The Japanese model proved to be flawed; in the 1990s Japan was gripped by an unrelenting recession that lasted for more than a decade. Japanese businesses were slowly forced to adopt American practices, including widespread layoffs, anathema to Japanese society until just recently.

Beginning in the 1970s, major change began to affect the performance and very existence of American companies in virtually every industry. Several bellwether events initiated the era of radical business change in America:

1. The creation of the OPEC cartel in 1973 and the first global energy crisis,

2. The deregulation of the airline industry in 1979, and

3. The forced breakup of AT&T in 1984, followed by
   deregulation of the telecommunications industry in 1994,
   which led to the growth of the Internet.

The energy crisis of 1973 showed that the organization of a previously fractious group of underdeveloped petroleum-exporting countries could create overnight a crisis that would severely disrupt business performance and profitability. OPEC also demonstrated that U.S. government foreign policy could no longer be conducted in a vacuum. Foreign policy decisions now affected American business and consumers, since OPEC's actions to cut off oil production had a dramatic impact on the U.S. economy. American companies quickly realized that their traditional planning and decision-making models could not account for an unpredictable event such as the oil cutoff. This was not just a failure of American business management, it was a failure of corporate culture, especially cultures that were rigid, inflexible, and bureaucratic. They could not anticipate the effects of that particular change force, and they were unable to react quickly and effectively.

The rise of Japanese quality production in the 1970s served as a less radical, but relentless change force on the American auto manufacturing industry, and it has had ripple effects across many manufacturing sectors. Japanese auto companies are now entrenched in the American economy and will soon overtake their steadily declining American competitors.

The deregulation of the airline industry was a goal eagerly pursued by that industry's leaders and proved a perfect example of the adage "Beware of what you wish for lest you get it." Had airline industry planners and decision makers truly understood how the competitive landscape would change, they might not have so eagerly lobbied for deregulation. *Today, the airline industry's culture, and its management, are obsolete.* Before deregulation, industry revenue was supported by government regulations. Now air carriers are propped up by too-willing investors and debt holders. The legacy carriers, like Delta and United, are saddled with outdated hub-and-spoke systems, but they also are held back by outdated "legacy" cultures that refuse to change in response to the new competitive realities of the industry.

The breakup of AT&T had similar unforeseen consequences for the telecom industry as well as the larger economy. In fact, the forced divestiture of the Baby Bells (the former regional operating units of AT&T) created an entirely new industry that had previously consisted of just one company—AT&T. It was upstart MCI's constant legal challenges that forced the breakup into seven independent regional telecom companies along with MCI, GTE, and Contel (none of which exists today). Further deregulation in 1994 accelerated the change within the industry. Interestingly, the newly formed Baby Bells feared that without long-distance service as a product offering, they would succumb to AT&T. Today, MCI and AT&T have failed and no longer exist as independent businesses. AT&T lost its sense of mission and never changed its culture after divestiture and later deregulation. MCI's famous culture, built on excellent service, innovation, and flexibility, was ruined by Bernie Ebbers, a former real estate developer, who looted the company, depriving it of the resources required to continue as a strong service company. Even after Ebbers was forced out, new management failed to rekindle its former culture of dedicated customer service and effective management.

RADICAL CHANGE AND CORPORATE CULTURE

Companies with high-performing cultures have the ability to anticipate change or respond effectively to change. Some of these companies actually create change. I call them New Age cultures. *Companies with underperforming cultures quickly lose market share and are the first to fail when confronted by radical change.* The last two decades of the twentieth century were marked by significant industry consolidation as many companies with poorly performing cultures became takeover targets or failed outright. The failure rate of companies between 1980 and 2000 outpaced the failure rate for the first eighty years of the twentieth century, according to the U.S. Department of Commerce.

The twenty-first century has seen no letup in the pace and impact of radical change. In fact, it may be said that one of the first new radical change forces of the twenty-first century was the burst bubble of an

industry that barely existed just ten years earlier—the Internet or dot
.com industry. Most business leaders were surprised by how closely
their companies' fortunes were tied to the dot.com phenomenon, especially telecom companies. More than $7 billion was lost by telecom
companies alone in the wake of the dot.com crash of 2001–2003.
Failed companies in this new industry forced a major downturn in the
entire economy as well as the failure of many other businesses, to the
tune of nearly a trillion dollars in lost revenue. Companies that were directly dependent upon the new Internet industry were severely affected,
and Silicon Valley, by itself, has experienced a likely permanent loss of
25 percent of its high-tech jobs since 2000. Software and gear-making
companies such as Cisco Systems, Sun Microsystems, Lucent, and
Nortel Networks lost significant revenue and market value. Lucent was
acquired by Alcatel after downsizing two-thirds of its workforce, and
Nortel hovers on the brink of failure. Once high-flying industry leaders
like Cisco and Sun Micro systems that had never experienced a downturn sustained major shocks to shareholders, employees, and their cultures. At Sun, which at one time had a market value that made it a
Fortune 20 company, no one had anticipated anything other than continued spectacular growth. Suddenly the company faced major downsizing. Just as the stale, outdated culture of the airline industries failed
to anticipate the effects of change, the fast-moving (and sometimes
chaotic) technology-focused cultures of Internet-related companies
never anticipated a possible downturn or planned ways to deal with its
consequences.

The radical change of the 1980s and 1990s seems modest by comparison to the radical change of the twenty-first century. The last
twenty years have seen the failure or near failure of companies that
were once icons of American business: Compaq, Motorola, Xerox,
United Airlines, Sunbeam, Columbia/HCA, Chrysler, Kodak, Ford,
Sears, Enron, Polaroid, AT&T, and Bethlehem Steel are just a few. In
addition, the entire American auto manufacturing industry and the domestic airline industry have, at one time or another, been on the brink
of failure, with the futures of General Motors and Ford now in serious
doubt. All of these companies had one thing in common—*the failure of
their corporate cultures*. Investors, boards, management, and employees

all believed that they had the right product or the right strategy—and still they failed. *What they did not have was the right culture.*

Entirely new business cultures have to be conceived, built, and managed for companies to ensure sustained success. Old command-and-control cultures built around inflexible and outdated hierarchies no longer work. In today's business environment, there are only one or two successful companies in most industries, and the other companies struggle just to remain in the game or hope to be acquired. Most of those companies will become pieces of property to be continually sold, traded, or mined for specific limited assets until those assets are exhausted. Andrew Grove, retired CEO and chairman of Intel, was quoted as saying, "It's not that American technology companies are getting less smart, but that the rest of the technology world is getting smarter, faster." Technology companies now have to start investing in their cultures the way they have invested in new technology if they are to maintain their competitive advantages.

THE HIERARCHY OF BUSINESS CHANGE FORCES

The notion of change in the business world has become diffuse and murky in the minds of many business leaders, managers, and workers. That, in turn, makes it difficult to create a connection between business change and culture change. There are many change forces at work today, and they tend to fall into three categories. *First-order change* comes primarily from the business world itself, regulatory agencies, global competitive change forces, and domestic and global economic trends. *Second-order change* is generated, in large part, by exploding new technology, scientific breakthroughs, and political and social change forces. *Third-order change* arises from changing demographics, labor and talent market shifts, and the consumer market.

Figure 1.1 Hierarchy of Change Forces

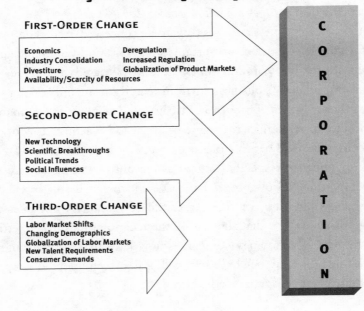

FIRST-ORDER CHANGE

Economics	Deregulation
Industry Consolidation	Increased Regulation
Divestiture	Globalization of Product Markets
Availability/Scarcity of Resources	

SECOND-ORDER CHANGE

New Technology
Scientific Breakthroughs
Political Trends
Social Influences

THIRD-ORDER CHANGE

Labor Market Shifts
Changing Demographics
Globalization of Labor Markets
New Talent Requirements
Consumer Demands

C O R P O R A T I O N

FIRST-ORDER CHANGE

First-Order Change forces include changing economic conditions, in-dustry consolidation, divestiture, deregulation, increased regulation, and globalization of markets. These change forces, large in scale, are what I call macro change forces.

GLOBAL COMPETITION LIKE NEVER BEFORE

Through the early twentieth century, competition was limited within regions such as Western Europe, North America, and small parts of South America and Asia. As American companies began to dominate certain industries, foreign companies and their governments began to do business with American companies on American terms, and that in-cluded having to use the English language. Not until the mid- to late-twentieth century did competition become truly global. Nations once underdeveloped are now growing robust companies that effectively compete with American companies across a wide range of industries. In high technology and communications, Taiwan, India, and South Korea have become centers of engineering and technology excellence. American companies and universities are no longer the sole source of innovation and high-technology development. The centers for auto, steel, software development, and biopharmaceutical design and development are now dispersed among many nations. Aircraft design and development are no longer controlled in America as European and Brazilian companies now rival Boeing and U.S. manufacturers of smaller aircraft. Through the North American Free Trade Agreement, its Central American counterpart, and the emergence (and recent expansion) of the European Union, entirely new economic trading blocs are emerging that compete on an equal footing with the United States. As a result, Microsoft must abide by new rules in Europe, not just America, and Boeing is no longer the world's preeminent aircraft manufacturer. A once lowly steel producer that utilizes scrap, Nucor, rose to become the dominant American steel producer, while most of the remaining steel industry has gone bankrupt. Japanese companies have had to offshore much of their manufacturing capacity to southeast Asian countries (in large part due to a demographic crisis of near-zero or falling population growth) while still expanding their auto manufacturing in America. With the fall of Soviet communism, a dozen new free economies have emerged in the former Eastern Bloc, while Russia has created a quasi-free economy built extensively on its rich oil and mineral resources, which are in ever-increasing demand around the globe by newly industrialized nations, especially China.

We have also seen the introduction of a new global currency, the euro, that rivals the U.S. dollar and Japanese yen. In just two generations, China has become the manufacturing workshop of the world as well as an emerging economic power. Fifty years ago, the United States was the main industrial power on the planet while China and India were preindustrial societies that frequently faced famine. The world no longer beats a path solely to American companies; American companies are having to go to the world, all the while facing tremendous foreign competition here at home. Much of this increased global competitiveness has been created by the fall of Soviet communism and by America itself, as we have continually urged foreign governments to create free and open markets.

INDUSTRY CONSOLIDATION

Industry consolidation has become a constant change factor in the business world. It is caused principally by two elements: excess capacity, as seen in the steel and airline industries, and companies' unwillingness to invest the time or money to grow market share organically. In many industries, radical change no longer makes it feasible to grow organically. If a company wants to expand its market share, it simply buys its competitors, regardless of size. According to Ernst & Young, there were 19,000 "major" mergers between 1991 and 2000 in the United States alone. Neither is industry consolidation limited to domestic markets, as mergers now take place between companies on different continents. Neither language, nor differing societal or business cultures, nor politics are an impediment to mergers. Industry consolidation has also been the major driving force behind the rise of the international corporation. Even Chinese companies are now in the hunt for foreign companies, as seen in the acquisition by Lenovo of IBM's personal computer operations, which has become an overnight computer technology force within China, preventing Dell from making major inroads in the Chinese marketplace. With the passing of the dot.com–induced recession, companies are now, more than ever, in the hunt for new acquisitions. This has a significant impact on workforces and business cultures, which will be discussed in detail in chapter 3.

DIVESTITURE

No divestiture can match the scale or consequences of the breakup of AT&T in 1984 into seven new Fortune 500 companies (of which only three now remain). Today the overwhelming trend is toward corporate combinations. Nevertheless, divestiture remains a necessity when wholly-owned subsidiaries no longer meet financial expectations of the larger holding company. This may include the burden of high overhead that the holding company no longer wishes to bear. It may also result from a previously failed acquisition, many times due to an incompatibility between cultures. Examples of this are AT&T's divestiture of previously acquired NCR and General Electric's acquisition and divestiture of Kidder Peabody. NCR had a company tradition as old as AT&T's, but it had a more focused and competitive business culture. This did not mix well with AT&T's slow-moving, highly bureaucratic culture, which grew out of many years of state and federal regulation. It was but one of many failed acquisitions that Michael Armstrong made while running AT&T. In its acquisition of Kidder Peabody, GE was unaware of widespread wrongdoing within Kidder Peabody's culture that forced GE to incur hundreds of millions of dollars in fines and legal fees. GE spun off the troubled investment bank within five years of acquiring it, and at a loss. A more recent example was seen in American Express's spin-off of Ameriprise, its investment banking arm that failed to live up to expectations for revenue growth. Much of the source of that failed marriage was due to the lack of synergies that American Express expected when originally making the purchase. Ameriprise must now go it alone, in an industry that is dominated by fewer but much larger competitors having deeper pockets.

But a divestiture is not automatically guaranteed to work. Many newly independent companies fail to redefine and rebuild their cultures, develop a new sense of identity, and instill new performance standards for the culture. The Bell companies failed to do this after their spin-off from AT&T, and for years floated aimlessly as clones of AT&T with cultures that failed to differentiate themselves from the old, failed AT&T culture. As a result, four of the original Baby Bells failed— along with AT&T. NYNEX, for instance, was technically bankrupt and petitioned Bell Atlantic to buy it to avoid failure.

DEREGULATION

Pressures to deregulate have come, principally, from industries themselves. Previously regulated industries, ranging from airlines and telecom to power generation and distribution, have all become deregulated and almost always with painful, if not disastrous, outcomes. While functioning in fully regulated environments, the regulated companies were characterized by bureaucratic cultures whose major responsibilities were to comply with regulations. In return, regulated companies were guaranteed either territories or price floors for their products and services, insulating them from failure. The widespread missteps and failures that have been experienced by companies in these industries are due, in large part, to their failure to change their cultures to meet the demands of a more competitive business environment. Many of the companies that failed became takeover targets for other companies.

INCREASED REGULATION

While much attention has been given to deregulation in recent years, increased regulation has been on the march, especially in the financial services sector. Interestingly, this has occurred during the era of a probusiness Congress and White House. Increased regulation is designed to ensure fairness of markets, safety, and reliability. The investment banking, stock brokerage, insurance, and mutual fund industries have all been subjected to increased scrutiny, litigation, and regulation. CEOs of major companies have been forced to resign or have even been indicted and convicted of fraudulent practices. These fraudulent practices have not been limited to CEOs alone, as bid rigging and market fixing have occurred deep within organizations, as seen at Enron and Marsh & McLennan, supposedly without the knowledge of their superiors. This behavior reflects predatory cultures at work to the detriment of the companies and the marketplace. A number of companies outside the financial services sector have resorted to financial misstatements to inflate the value of their stock, reduce loan rates for borrowing, and increase the compensation of a handful of officers at the very top of the organization.

The recent wave of increased regulation has occurred on both the federal and state levels. At the federal level, the Justice Department, Securities and Exchange Commission, and the Federal Trade Commission have been increasingly active in imposing new oversight regulations to ensure fairer markets. The Sarbanes-Oxley Act, a major piece of federal regulation, was passed by Congress to protect investors against fraudulent financial reporting by corporations. In many cases, the states actually anticipated the federal government in their regulatory efforts, as seen in Connecticut, Alabama, and, most conspicuously, New York, through the state attorney general's office run by Eliot Spitzer.

Regulatory control is also evident in protecting the environment, enforcing workplace safety, and preventing employment discrimination. Virtually all industries have demanded fewer controls and regulations while waging relentless campaigns against OSHA, EPA, SEC, and the EEOC. *If American businesses want fewer outside controls and oversight, they need to create cultures that will be vigilant in monitoring their own in-house conduct and business practices, and more proactive in preventing malfeasance while promoting the best professional practices. This requires that companies build performance-driven, ethical cultures.*

CHANGING ECONOMIC CONDITIONS

Ever-changing economic forces may be the ultimate agents of change in the competitive business environment. These may occur as recessions within an industry or a nation or on a global scale. Economic change may be created by restricting or expanding the supply of a widely required natural resource or by changing the supply of money by national central banking systems. These all have effects on industries as well as national economies. With the increasing interdependence of national economies, these change forces have a global impact. Of course, economic depressions are the most extreme change forces.

SECOND-ORDER CHANGE

Second Order Change is driven by social and political change forces as well as by technological and scientific breakthroughs.

Scientific and Technological Change

Scientific and technological breakthroughs have been a major force for driving change for the past twenty years and have spawned brand-new industries, not just new companies. These range from new software development to new communications devices (dependent upon software) and the most exotic scientific discoveries in the fields of biopharmaceuticals and medicine. IBM, Microsoft, and Apple are widely recognized as the progenitors of the age of computers, especially for their wider application to consumer markets. Apple and Microsoft, once considered true New Age businesses, are now deemed mature companies with the advent of even newer companies like eBay and Google that have found entirely new ways to use the Internet.

Biomedical breakthroughs have also created significant change and spawned entirely new industries in the fields of medical devices, biomedicine, and genetic engineering. The new medical device industry has given rise to Fortune 500 companies Medtronic and Boston Scientific. The biomedical sector is dominated by $10 billion Amgen, the first such company in this field, along with Baxter, Amgen, and Novartis. Biomedical companies have become indispensable partners with and contributors to the pharmaceutical industry. Virtually every pharmaceutical company has formed an alliance with a biopharmaceutical company or purchased one. Human Genome Sciences in suburban Washington, D.C., has become the "Amgen" of the even newer realm of human genome research. Around it has grown a biomedical corridor in Maryland similar to the high-technology corridors in suburban Boston, Northern Virginia, and Silicon Valley. These will be the New Age industries of the twenty-first century that replace nineteenth- and twentieth-century manufacturing and distribution industries.

Social and Political Change

Ever-changing social and political currents have always had a profound impact on business. Changes in political parties at the local, state, and federal levels impact business. Many of the regulatory change forces, discussed earlier, are the products of political change. Social change forces also have an impact on business.

Not to be ignored as a source of political and social change is the business sector itself. Specific industries exert tremendous influence on the state and federal government. In so-called company towns, companies have been known to wield significant social and political influence to the point of putting towns out of business when they close plants, offices, and distribution centers that were the major employers in the locality.

THIRD-ORDER CHANGE

Third-Order Change affects the nature of work, as well as workers. Many manufacturing jobs have permanently left the United States, forcing the larger question: "What will American society do as it loses much of its traditional employment base?" This includes service jobs such as call centers, which are increasingly being offshored to countries with large English-speaking labor pools, such as India and the Philippines.

Neither can it be assumed that high-level technology professions will be protected. There are recent indications that knowledge-based jobs are being offshored to Asia and even Eastern Europe, where the cost of talent is lower. Microsoft in 2005 moved eighty-five software architect positions to Asia—positions considered to be at the top of the technology talent pyramid. In addition, companies are bringing less costly technology talent from Asia to the United States, many times under State Department rules that allow such talent to be paid less than local talent.

Nevertheless, American companies cannot assume that they can always go to foreign markets for a ready pool of less costly knowledge and management talent. As the economies of India and China grow, they create new businesses that have their own increasing needs for well-trained and well-educated talent as well as for semiskilled talent. While the pay scales of indigenous companies are lower than those of American companies, wages are rapidly increasing and are expected eventually to match the compensation offered by American companies in overseas markets. American companies doing business overseas may eventually find that overseas labor cost advantages will disappear. In addition, there is the factor of increasing nationalistic pride. American companies may become employers of second choice as Asian nationals are starting to give their loyalty first to employers from their own countries.

Before offshoring, outsourcing also contributed to dislocations in the labor market as companies shed in-house production and distribution overhead and capabilities to outsourcing companies that were willing to provide the same service with reduced costs for labor and benefits. This meant that workers had to bear the burden of these reductions in overhead through lower pay and reduced or eliminated benefits of their outsourcing employers. Outsourcing has encompassed blue-collar manufacturing jobs and white-collar positions in human resources and information technology management. For example, many companies have completely outsourced their human resource functions to firms that handle the personnel needs for several companies. The major IT consulting firms, including the Big Four accounting firms, manage the in-house IT needs of large corporations.

Technology has also contributed to the elimination of many clerical and administrative jobs. Many former secretarial responsibilities are now handled by managers through the use of more powerful computing resources and advanced communications devices. That in turn has changed the traditional role of the secretary to that of an administrator and information manager, and there are far fewer of them in most companies today than fifteen or even five years ago.

Sooner, rather than later, American companies (and labor unions) will have to take their heads out of the sand to develop proactive employment policies that will be mutually beneficial to both employers and employees.

CHANGING DEMOGRAPHICS

Changing demographics constitutes a gradual but lasting change force on American business and corporate cultures. Like other advanced economies, America is producing fewer American-born engineers, scientists, physicians, medical researchers, and business managers. Part of this is due to slowing population growth in affluent societies compared with developing nations. This has affected not just American businesses, but also American universities. To fill the gap, universities have admitted more students from abroad, especially from countries like India, China, Indonesia, Thailand, and South Korea, which lack the institutions of higher learning needed to train their burgeoning populations. That, combined with the overall aging of our population, is creating major gaps in expertise and talent within American companies. The increasing rate of retirement of the Baby Boomers, in particular, has left many careers and professions short of white-collar professionals. We need only look at Japan and Italy to see the effects of an aging population on business. Japan is now experiencing zero population growth. Since the Japanese society has remained closed to immigration, Japanese companies have been forced to offshore production to other Asian nations that have younger and rapidly growing populations. Beginning in 1999, more Japanese autos were being manufactured outside Japan than inside the country. Italy is a rapidly aging nation with a negative population growth rate. Once known for its engineering and design prowess, Italy has fallen behind other countries in these disciplines. It has also had to allow the temporary immigration of large numbers of semiskilled and unskilled workers to fill blue-collar jobs. American companies are starting to employ foreign nationals for key jobs, especially in overseas locations. As American companies increase their presence in other nations, they hire foreign professionals who can bridge the language and cultural gap and who work for wages that are lower than in America, but still considered high for those societies.

CONSUMERS

Consumers also provide a source of change for the business world. In the wake of ever-larger companies, many bemoan the fact that consumers no longer have as much clout as they once did. Consumer choices have become more limited as the consolidation of industries around fewer companies provides fewer choices for products and services. Nevertheless, consumers have still shown an ability to exert their concerns, complaints, and influence. The Internet has been a true democratizing instrument and a megaphone for discontent. When Dell computer was widely criticized by its customers over the Internet for its persistently poor customer support, its leaders finally recognized the need to improve its after-sales service and support. Investors who lost money due to malfeasance by investment banks and insurance companies revolted and forced stricter oversight and increased regulation. This was accomplished by exerting political pressure on regulators and their political representatives. Again, the Internet was an effective tool in making their needs known.

CORPORATE CULTURE AND THE BUSINESS CHANGE CYCLE

Business enterprises, as dynamic systems, are highly complex, frequently unpredictable, and difficult to change. When combined with the volatile change forces arising in the marketplace, they become even

Figure 1.2 Business Change Cycle

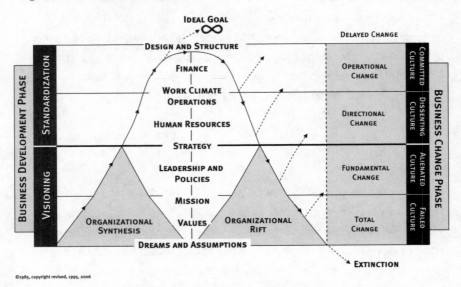

©1985, copyright revised, 1995, 2006

Figure 1.2 (Read from bottom left to top and down the right side.)

more challenging to lead. Companies do not grow and develop in a straight line. All companies, indeed entire industries, experience an uneven ebb and flow as they first emerge, develop, grow, experience various levels of change, and eventually go out of existence. Change cycles help to chart and understand companies as they move through these various change stages. The *Business Change Cycle* serves as a means of looking at a company's internal functioning in response to change as well as a guide to where it needs to go. Unlike most other change cycles that typically deal with just one or two dimensions of a company's functioning, this change cycle tracks a broad range of different company dimensions, including the business formation phases, various change stages, internal business functions, as well as the performance of the culture.

CORPORATE CULTURE AND THE EMERGING NEW BUSINESS: THE BUSINESS DEVELOPMENT PHASE

We sometimes forget that all of today's major corporations were once just a dream in a visionary founder's mind. This is true even for the sometimes overwhelming and frequently bureaucratic cultures of large, long-established companies. But where did the cultures come from, and how were they formed? Gates, Moore and Noyce, Chambers, Case, Ford, Hewlett and Packard, Olson, McGowan, Galvin, and Westinghouse had modest beginnings as visionaries, but they were able to grow their ambitious plans into corporate giants. Some of those founders, like William Hewlett and David Packard of Hewlett-Packard and William McGowan of MCI, took great care to identify and develop a particular type of culture that they felt was needed to support the growth and long-term success of their fledging new companies.

Unfortunately, most founders fail to think about the kind of culture that will best serve the strategic goals of the new business, and they give even less attention to how to build the culture that will support those goals. Many times, this leads to the premature failure of an emerging new company or, at the very least, permits the culture to take on a life of its own that may not be responsive to the strategic direction set for the company.

CORPORATE VISIONING

At the bottom left of the Business Change Cycle, where companies are first born, there is a gray wedge identified as Organizational Synthesis. As a new company is coming together, it is critical that a visioning process be undertaken to formalize the focus, values, identity, purpose, commitments, standards for ethical conduct, behaviors, performance standards, and leadership requirements for the new company that are needed for its success. These are especially important, as most companies in this stage have few of the formal operating components and little of the structure that start to emerge in the standardization stage and are always seen in fully mature companies. This formative stage of the new company's development is an excellent opportunity for the founder to clarify his vision for the company as well as its culture—which can either make or break the emergent company. *This is where the new culture starts to form and is best managed and directed by leadership. At no other time will the founder be able to exercise greater leadership over the culture-building process.*

As the emerging new business moves up the development side of the change curve, the mission serves as a platform for developing new leadership and management. Without the mission, leadership is in a fog. In addition, new policies need to be developed that will serve as a guide for day-to-day functioning of everyone within the company. Again, without a clear mission, policies become nothing more than a set of bureaucratic do's and don'ts.

BUSINESS STANDARDIZATION

Business standardization arises from the need to formalize business operations and practices so that the new company can effectively and reliably satisfy growing customer demands for its products and services. This positive development indicates to management that the company is beginning to create a critical mass—an absolute necessity for sustained success and continued growth. *Too often, new companies get caught up in the make and sell cycle in response to increasing demand for its products.*

Mushrooming staffing levels frequently accompany increased demand for products and services. In an effort to keep up, management overlooks critical issues related to the culture. This can spell trouble for the new company's survival. Management cannot afford to bring large numbers of new employees into the organization with their own notions and past experiences about culture. The outcome will be that the new workforce creates its own culture. Hiring people for their individual skills and capabilities is not enough. Management needs to proactively engage in systematic culture-building processes to make clear what kind of culture the company will have and not let it evolve on its own into a culture that can incubate future problems. This will make a critical difference in how the company conducts business in the marketplace; whether it has a formal and recognized set of standards for conduct; or whether it is left up to individual employees or special groups and cliques within the company. In many cases, people with strong career ambitions will start to exercise excessive careerist behaviors at the expense of others in an effort to quickly get to the top of the new company. If the founders of the company have clearly defined the culture that is needed during the *visioning* stage and started the culture-building process during that period, then the new company will more likely grow through new hires who will be committed to the long-term success and growth of the company.

Too often, the management of companies in this stage of development will have a tendency to take advantage of new hires (and contractors) to help grow the company, while not giving them a stake in the company's future success. When this happens, employees are more likely to take advantage of the company by taking proprietary technology and clients with them to competitors or using them in their own start-up plans. This frequently occurs when the emerging new company hits inevitable downturns. If a company is not able to overcome inevitable setbacks and downturns at this stage of its development, it will remain trapped in the development phase of the change cycle or it will fail.

![CASE STUDY banner]

[CASE STUDY]

A Twenty-Year-Old Company Stuck in the Development Phase of the Change Cycle

IBTCI was founded in 1986 by one family which continues to control this professional services firm today. Its principal objective has always been to provide technical and financial consulting to the governments of emerging new countries and their central banks. IBTCI wins contracts from various U.S. government agencies (e.g., USAID), international government (United Nations) and nongovernmental agencies (World Bank and International Monetary Fund), as well as from large commercial firms that subcontract to smaller firms. IBTCI competes in a highly competitive marketplace that has a growing list of new competitors each year. Nevertheless, the owner continues to see the company and its competitive environment as it was twenty years earlier.

The firm employs well-educated professionals from such disciplines as economics, accounting, international law, security, and information technology. About half of its workforce is composed of full-time, permanent employees who are supplemented by contract workers hired for specific long-term projects. IBTCI has gone through a number of painful ups and downs linked to larger economic trends and global political events. During downturns, the firm may lose up to two-thirds of its revenues while profit margins completely disappear, forcing it to reduce staff accordingly.

During these downturns, the firm cuts or completely eliminates internal support functions, including its human resource function (usually, in such circumstances, an employee is asked to step in to run human resources and carry out his normal duties). As a result human resources is generally used only to process the hiring and dismissal of employees. The personnel policy manual has not been updated for more than twelve years and is a catalog of don'ts. The performance appraisal process is a highly subjective, top-down process that lacks quantification while failing to include the employees or coworkers in the evaluation process. In addition, its health-care plan is outdated and fails to cover employees who are overseas for more than thirty days. Human resources at IBTCI does not meet current professional standards.

Client relations and new technology development are critical to the firm's ongoing success. The CEO strictly controls all activities and makes almost all important decisions for staff even though most employees are stationed in far-off countries most of the time. As a result, employees quickly learn to not take too much individual initiative, especially since they infrequently share in the rewards of increased revenues and profits. Promotions are rare, and top positions are reserved for family members or filled through outside hiring made by the family, not through internal merit promotion. Few opportunities arise for employees to commit to the company and its clients on a long-term basis, and their ideas are usually mined by the owners. As one employee noted, "Effective, current management practices are unheard-of here."

When the company does go into a downturn, laid-off or disaffected employees take proprietary technology and clients with them to competitors or to support the start-up of their own ventures. This means that IBTCI is sponsoring much of its new competition. The company seems to be caught in a never-ending boom-and-bust cycle while being caught in the bottom quadrant of the Business Change Cycle.

IBTCI is a company that will probably never create critical mass or reach its full potential. It lacks a systematic strategy that will allow it to grow into a fully functioning company. Just as important, it lacks a well-defined culture that will foster mutual commitment between employees and the company. This is essential if the company is to effectively compete in a radically changed business climate—a business climate that is quite different from the one that existed when it was founded nearly twenty years earlier. IBTC is not an employer of choice and does not earn employee commitment or loyalty.

Newer and smaller companies are most often associated with the business development phase of the change cycle, but not always. Companies that are spun off from a large corporate entity or are the product of a merger of relative equals also find themselves on this side of the change cycle. Too often, management of the new business entity acts as if it is "business as usual," which causes it to miss a critical opportunity to redefine the mission and culture while creating a corporate identity that is distinct from its former business affiliation. In other cases, like IBTCI, we see long-established companies that never create enough critical mass to justify their moving beyond the development phase of the business change cycle—due in large part to their failure to define and develop a culture that will attract and keep top talent.

CORPORATE CULTURE AND THE CHANGE PHASE OF THE BUSINESS CHANGE CYCLE

The goal of all companies is to grow and develop without experiencing the change phase of the Business Change Cycle. Today, companies such as Johnson & Johnson, Nucor, Latex International, and Intuit are able to sustain peak performance for prolonged periods without experiencing the downside of the change cycle (see Figure 4). AT&T and Fannie Mae are examples of two companies that experienced sustained peak performance for many decades without experiencing the change phase of the business cycle. They accomplished that feat in large part because of their protected status as regulated companies, which provided artificial protection from normal competitive conditions. That, in turn, created cultures that were bureaucratic, risk-averse, and accountable more to government regulators than to the marketplace. The breakup of AT&T, followed by partial deregulation of the telecom industry, precipitated a twenty-year decline for the former telecom giant with its demise in 2005. Once a Fortune 10, $100-billion-plus corporation, AT&T had revenues of approximately $36 billion at the time of its purchase by SBC.

Fannie Mae was chartered by Congress and, along with Freddie Mac, was protected from normal competitive pressures in order to create fair and stable mortgage markets. The recent troubles at both companies can be directly attributed to their cultures of hubris. They saw themselves as being too big and important to be brought down. Investigations revealed that both companies were financially overextended while management manipulated and misstated their financial positions. It cost both companies their senior management teams. More important, if either company had failed, the country's economy could have been wrecked, or, at the least, we taxpayers would have had to bail out the mortgage markets just as we had done when the thrift industry collapsed.

Companies that function in relatively nonregulated markets have also been able to sustain peak performance for prolonged periods. Examples include IBM until the 1980s, GE during the Jack Welch era, Southwest Airlines, and today's oil-producing industry.

But regardless of size, resources, proprietary technology, pools of talent, or leadership acumen, all companies eventually experience the change phase of the business change cycle.

DELAYED CHANGE

Delayed change reflects a temporary suspension of normal business conditions. It is no longer clear what direction the company will be taking, and it cannot be plotted on the Business Change Cycle. This may be caused by a major crisis within the company that requires everyone's attention. A natural disaster or a crisis such as the World Trade Center attack is the sort of event that forces the suspension of normal operations. A more common cause is a change in the leadership of a company. Here a good example would be Jack Welch's retirement from GE. While his retirement was anticipated and Jeffrey Immelt emerged as his replacement from GE's succession-planning process, the company was, in effect, frozen on the delayed change line on the change curve. People within the company, markets, and investors waited to determine whether Immelt would take the corporation in a different direction or his leadership style would make an impact on the company's culture. From 2001 to 2005, Research in Motion, Inc., maker of the groundbreaking Blackberry communications device, was also stuck at the delayed change phase of the change cycle because of legal challenges to its technology. It finally settled the case in March 2006.

OPERATIONAL CHANGE

Operational change is the most common form of business change. All companies experience operational change—it's normal. Companies are always looking for better ways to improve productivity, enhance cycle time, control costs, and maintain quality. Common conditions that reflect the need for operational change include:

- Production inefficiencies
- Distribution problems
- Customer dissatisfaction
- Quality control deficits
- Escalating production costs
- Safety issues

Common strategies that are employed in response to these conditions include:

- Better cost accounting and control
- Productivity improvement
- Improved safety guidelines
- Work climate enhancement
- Workforce training and education
- Improved customer service
- New technology implementation
- Supply chain management measures (e.g., JIT)
- Overhead budget management
- Introduction of quality improvement measures
- Improved or restructured operations

The need for operational change measures has always been common in manufacturing and transportation, but they are also important to service companies, especially those that are built around call centers, as well as companies that are transaction-based, such as insurance companies and banks.

When a company experiences operational change, the culture remains strongly committed to the business. Employees see it as a normal part of their responsibilities to help improve various operational deficits. Businesses that have high-performing cultures frequently trust their employees to identify and implement necessary operational improvements without excessive management oversight or bureaucratic policy making. Two such companies are Nucor Steel and Harley-Davidson. The managements of those companies know that their frontline employees are closer to the customer and better understand customer needs.

DIRECTIONAL CHANGE

When a company is experiencing directional change, its strategy is no longer effective in the marketplace and the business is losing market share. Directional change arises for a number of reasons, including:

- Improved products and services by competitors
- Regulatory or legal constraints
- New, more capable competitors in a company's traditional market space (often from overseas)
- The inability of a company's culture to support a new strategic direction
- A mismatch between a company's human resources and new strategic initiatives
- Lagging research and development
- Improved technologies that give a competitor the edge

One factor that allowed Wal-Mart to overtake Kmart was its utilization of modern just-in-time (JIT) supply-chain technology. JIT allowed it to instantly track product inventory at any point in its vast worldwide distribution system and within each store. Until 2004, Kmart was still tied to decades-old warehouse inventory replenishment practices. In addition, Kmart did not even have e-mail communications between corporate headquarters and its regional offices and stores until 2001. Kmart was left standing still while Wal-Mart became the largest consumer retailer in the world. How a company uses technology reveals a lot about a company's culture.

Culture has a major impact on a company's ability to successfully implement strategy. While telecom-industry upstarts Ericsson and Nokia were solidly committed to digital standards for a new generation of wireless communications devices, industry leader Motorola was bogged down by internal political warfare over whether to use analog or digital technology. Its reliance on old analog technology cost it market share that it may never win back. More critically, the company was not able to marshal its culture to support a single, focused strategic initiative in the marketplace.

When a company experiences directional change, pockets of dissent become more apparent as key people or departments within the business disagree with the existing strategy or newly proposed strategies. This is not necessarily unhealthy. To the contrary, a company that undertakes a new strategy without allowing critical feedback from the culture will make itself and the strategy vulnerable to failure.

Necessary strategies for responding to directional change include:

- Developing a new business strategy which leads operational strategy
- Exploiting competitor weaknesses and marketplace opportunities
- Redefining the company's market niche
- Improving R&D
- Changing human resource strategy to support business strategy
- Encouraging widespread feedback, risk taking, and innovation
- Evaluating the company's culture and aligning it to support the company's new strategy

FUNDAMENTAL CHANGE

Fundamental change indicates that a company is starting to fail. The very fundamentals of the business, such as mission, leadership, and policies, are failing. Organizational rift and dysfunctionality are setting in (see Figure 1.3). When a company experiences fundamental change, *its leadership is failing and has lost the confidence and support of the company's culture. The culture is also alienated from leadership, its policies, and the company's mission, which effectively ceases to exist. The company's culture is becoming dysfunctional and, more ominously, is no longer committed to serving the customer. It may even be hostile to the customer.* Conditions reflecting fundamental change include:

- Obsolete mission and strategy
- *Alienated and failing culture*
- Failing and isolated leadership
- Increasing turnover in middle-management ranks
- Defections of key talent
- Customer defections

Necessary strategies for rescuing a company from the fundamental stage of change encompass:

- Implementation of a broad-based change strategy which leads business strategy
- Creating a new, more meaningful mission with widespread company buy-in
- *Changing the culture to support the change effort and rebuild company-wide commitment*
- Redefining talent requirements
- Reaching out to customers and other stakeholders for their input
- Developing and implementing a new business strategy
- Conducting an organization effectiveness audit and implementing an organization strategy to support the new business strategy
- Undertaking extensive leadership coaching or replacing the leadership team

It is a tremendous challenge to create and implement a successful change management strategy for a company when it is experiencing this level of change. Frequently, there are too many internal problems and deficits to overcome to return the company to renewed performance and growth. If the company is to regain its former level of performance and restored confidence among all of its stakeholders, the change effort (turnaround) must be *qualitative—not just quantitative.*

Restructuring and downsizing are strictly quantitative measures and will only shrink the scope of the problems or move then around. They will not resolve the fundamental problems facing the business. *Changing the culture must be at the core of any successful change effort.* To change the culture, a broad consensus-building effort that is inclusive of the entire organization must be undertaken.

Many companies experiencing this level of change are taken over by turnaround specialists who have little interest and less commitment to restoring the business to its former level of performance. Instead, they usually undertake draconian cost-cutting measures and mine the company for any strategic assets (proprietary technology) or key products. If anything is left, they may then sell the greatly diminished company, usually for its remaining physical assets, such as any real estate holdings or equipment.

TOTAL CHANGE

Total change foretells a company's imminent failure. Virtually all business systems are failing or have failed, but more important, the culture has totally failed. Stakeholders of the business recognize this and have long ago fled for the exits. Remaining workers and managers will actually sabotage the company by sharing proprietary company secrets or technology with competitors in hopes of gaining employment with them. They may also attempt to take customers to competitors to ensure their own employment, or they may try to lure customers to their own new business start-up ventures. The culture has long since failed and has become openly hostile to customers and the marketplace. Conditions reflecting total change include:

- Failed mission
- Failed strategy—no ability to compete in the marketplace
- Failed leadership
- *Failed culture*
- Failed values

Failed values, dreams, and assumptions of the founders or current leaders are a critical contributor to the failure of the company. Even if the business attempts to remain in existence, these underlying foundations for the business must be completely replaced or rebuilt.

It is almost impossible to save a company at this stage of the change cycle. If the effort is to be made, required change strategies must include:

- Creating an entirely new set of values, dreams, purposes, and assumptions about the business
- Reinventing the entire business (don't try to rebuild it on the ruins of the former business)
- Replacing the leadership and key managers (coaching of old leadership will not be successful)
- Placing culture building at the core of the new business creation process to build an entirely new culture
- Enlisting the support of new stakeholders for the planned new business
- Creating a new business strategy

Total change does not always reflect business failure but can be a product of planned total change. In some cases, a company's owners and leadership re-form the company into an entirely different type of business while translating it into new markets requiring entirely new business requirements to support this form of total change. The Westinghouse Corporation initiated a successful total-change effort in the 1990s and early twenty-first century by divesting itself of many of its heavy industrial businesses in favor of technology and media businesses such as its former media and broadcasting business.

American National Can was an excellent example of this type of total change. Originally a manufacturer of metal cans and other container products, the board decided to transform the company into a financial services and investment company that became known as Primerica Corporation. Figuring it did not require the overhead of a manufacturing company, the board sold off its plants at ninety cents on the dollar to a French consortium in order to fund the business transformation. Nevertheless, much of its original leadership and board remained in

Figure 1.3 Business Change Cycle

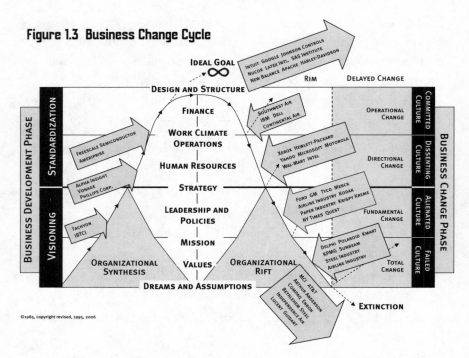

©1985, copyright revised, 1995, 2006

place. More telling, the new company failed to undertake a new corporate missioning and culture-building process. The company failed with the stock market collapse of 1987, and Sanford Weill added it to the portfolio of companies he was building into Citigroup.

Other companies have succeeded in the total change process. When the original vision of An Wang (the first developer of work-station technology) failed, Wang Labs saved itself by becoming a software developer. People today forget that Harley-Davidson and Chrysler successfully undertook the total change effort (albeit the latter with initial support from the government to protect it from predatory foreign competitors). Both companies based their turnarounds on completely new missions and corporate cultures, and both have retained unionized workforces. Chrysler is now a division of German DaimlerChrysler Corporation (outperforming its German parent), and Harley-Davidson is a highly profitable, premier manufacturing company once again. In fact, Harley-Davidson asked the government to remove the tariffs on foreign competitors as it believed and demonstrated that it could compete on its own.

Planned or unplanned, total change reflects the most serious challenge to a business's survival and possible renewal. Unplanned total change is frequently the product of a failed culture over a prolonged period, and without exception, failed culture is found in companies that are struggling with total change. Planned total change cannot succeed without putting culture at the center of the change process.

2

ILLUMINATING THE BLACK HOLE

Culture is one of the most precious things a company has, so you must work harder on it than anything else.

—Herb Kelleher, Founder, Southwest Airlines

Even when not ignored, corporate culture is, all too often, a mystifying subject for employees, managers, and leaders of most companies. While coaching a team of internal change agents for a consumer products distribution company, I probed the participants' thoughts and attitudes about their own company's corporate culture. Not surprisingly, their perceptions and experiences were widely varied, even though they were all employed within the same company. Finally, one team member volunteered that the company's culture was "like a black hole. Any new initiative we try to introduce just seems to be sucked up into it, never to be heard from again." This very frank description of the company's culture seemed to galvanize the change team. It gave them a common starting point for undertaking the culture change process. For too many of today's business enterprises, corporate culture drains too many resources, innovative ideas, and practices as well as employee initiative and commitment without company management knowing it.

Common Misconceptions About Corporate Culture

We need to come to grips with what the term "culture" means—and does not mean. Even among my colleagues in the consulting world, culture is something we can infer, talk about, and criticize, but few are able to define it in a way that directly relates to business performance. Academics tend to speak of corporate culture in psychological and sociological-anthropological terms. In fact, the term "culture" was first used by anthropologists to refer to the behaviors, qualities, and unique characteristics of any particular human group. More recently, the legal, regulatory, and media sectors see it only in more narrow terms of ethical and legal malfeasance. As a result, corporate culture has come to carry negative connotations in the minds of many in the business world. Many feel it refers to the "soft, touchy-feely" issues such as worker contentment and happiness, a pleasant work environment, or lavish perquisites for management and workers. When former Corning CEO Roger Ackerman decided to undertake the culture building process, he would not allow the term "corporate culture" to be used. Instead, he insisted that the term "operational environment" be used in its place (which seems to carry an entirely different meaning, related to the operations of the business). In reality, a company's culture has everything to do with bottom-line business performance based on the performance of its people. Work climate and ethical conduct are certainly contributors, but the culture is much more than that.

Here are two very different CEO perspectives on corporate culture as seen through the eyes of two chief executive officers.

[CASE STUDY]

A CEO's Failure to Come to Grips with Corporate Culture— and the Consequences

GXS, Inc., a pioneering $500 million enterprise-networking company, was losing market share after long leading its market sector. In recent years it had been spun off by several parent companies, including GE. I was called in by two senior officers to discuss their concerns, which they characterized as going beyond operational issues. They were certain that the company's culture was at the core of the problem, as it was experiencing increased customer defections, while the help desk function (critical to a company in that industry) was coming under growing criticism for its inability to satisfy client needs. It was unusual, but refreshing, for two officers to openly refer to the culture as a problem for the company. While not directly addressing clear-cut factors, they suspected two key causes: massive downsizing of its engineering and technical corps and large-scale offshoring of jobs to Asia to reduce overhead as demanded by the company's new venture-capital owners. As a result, clients lost track of reliable technical representatives on whom they had become dependent while feeling increasingly alienated from the company by its Asian technical support representatives. After spending several months to gain support from key managers and officers for a proposed plan to rebuild the culture, the two officers seemed reluctant to sign off on the proposal. It was clear that the CEO had to be included, and I suggested that we all meet together with him.

An expanded group of executives and I met for three hours with the CEO, a seemingly thoughtful man who had spent much of his career in various corporate general counsel roles but who had acquired a great deal of knowledge about the technology of the company and broader industry. Finally, at the conclusion of the discussion, he spun his chair around and looked out the window, seemingly in deep thought. We all sat in silence waiting for him to return to the discussion. Finally, he turned back to the table and said, "I think I've done a lot for the culture here." "What initiatives have you taken with the culture?" I asked. "Well, I put free sodas and snacks in the vending machines, and I opened a fitness center for the employees here at corporate." The chief human resources officer, sitting next to me, quietly shook his head in frustration while another officer grimaced. I was a little stunned by the CEO's response, but not terribly surprised. This was a typical response. Four months later, the CEO was dismissed, and the problems and customer defections continued to mount, all to the detriment of the company's bottom line.

At the other end of the continuum is the perspective of Louis Gerstner, the very successful (some would say heroic) CEO of IBM, who was so instrumental in that company's dramatic turnaround. Shortly after his retirement, Gerstner was interviewed on the *Charlie Rose Show*. One of Rose's questions to Gerstner was the following: "If you could tell CEOs what is the single most important thing they could do to ensure the long-term success of their companies, what would it be?" Without delay, Gerstner shot back, *"CEOs have to realize that corporate culture is not one thing they do in leading the company; it is everything they do."* That may well be one of the most enlightened statements on the subject of business culture that has ever been rendered. Indeed, under his leadership, Gerstner deemphasized the constant musical chairs of restructuring that has become so overused in the business world. Instead, he focused on a new strategy for the business in response to changing conditions in the marketplace, and he set about rebuilding the company's once famed culture to support the new strategy. This included putting people and resources together while breaking down the many organizational silos that had been putting roadblocks in the way of IBM's going to market and serving customers in a manner that had previously made IBM legendary. Throughout this book, we will examine other examples of companies that are getting the culture right and are thriving.

CORPORATE CULTURE DEFINED

Over the years, I have led numerous seminars for business groups and senior management teams and I like to give a pop quiz at the start of every session. One question I ask of the participants is to define corporate culture. The answers are usually varied and vague and generally reflect a lack of true understanding of the subject. Many of the participants' responses have to do with specific working conditions—the work climate; "the company's unconscious goals"; how they work together in teams; how people are treated; and, recently, ethical behavior. One of the more common responses I hear is "the way we do things." That answer, in particular, reflects how nebulous and difficult the subject is for people to grasp. I probe and challenge the audience to develop a definition that more directly addresses their individual and corporate performance, accountability, commitments, values, standards of behavior, as well as the rites and rituals of the company. My own definition over the years has been as follows:

"The collective belief systems that people within the organization have about their ability to compete in the marketplace—and how they act on those belief systems to bring value-added services and products to the marketplace (the customer) in return for financial reward. Corporate culture is revealed through the attitudes, belief systems, dreams, behaviors, values, rites, and rituals of the company, and most especially through the conduct and performance of its employees and management" (J. Want, *Managing Radical Change: Beyond Survival in the New Business Age,* Wiley, 1995). The key word in the definition is "and," as belief systems without action simply become empty slogans. The corporate world is famous for its many empty slogans.

Yes, work climate and perks are components of a company's larger culture. The employees at SAS Institute work in a veritable country club environment, which probably does contribute in some degree to employee commitment, if not performance, and to the company's larger success. They even have a concierge service to take care of employee needs and a gymnasium and pool on the campus. At the same time, electronics manufacturer Emerson Electric has long demonstrated that it maintains a high-performing and ethical culture, but its manufacturing work climate can be described as anything but a country club. In addition, compensation at Emerson is not fixed or guaranteed but is linked to the performance of the company. Despite that, employee turnover is extremely low.

At the other end of the scale, WorldCom's Bernie Ebbers was famous for making the work environment as uncomfortable and devoid of work resources as possible, mistakenly thinking that it would produce better bottom-line results. According to one executive, he went so far as to remove chairs from conference rooms and coffeemakers from canteens in hopes that their removal would reduce informal conferences and worker chat sessions.

CORPORATE CULTURE AND PERFORMANCE

Ultimately, the importance of corporate culture is linked directly to the ability of a company to effectively compete in a radically changing business climate. Too many corporate leaders and planners think that by putting together a new business plan the company will automatically fulfill that plan. They fail to take a good, hard look at the company's culture to see if it is capable of measuring up to the new strategy. More thoughtful business leaders recognize that corporate culture is *the* critical difference between companies becoming perpetual industry leaders or also-rans or outright failures. In the age of radical change there will be fewer distinctions made between the also-rans and failures. No company can expect to succeed with an underperforming culture. The business landscape is littered with failed companies—even failed industries—that were held back by their cultures. Southwest Bell wanted to move into the publishing industry with a nationwide yellow pages. That effort failed, in part, because they did not take into account the need for a different business culture that could meet the very different needs of thousands of different marketplaces around the country rather than just the familiar ones in their region of the country. Putting together a yellow pages directory also requires the ability to individualize for its many business client listings, a capability that is lacking in most bureaucratic cultures.

The former pharmaceutical giant SmithKline was a company that went through three different mergers, with each failing to meet its potential because of the company's failed culture. SmithKline was the first pharmaceutical company to develop and produce the first billion-dollar blockbuster drug—Tagamet. This revolutionary drug provided relief for millions who suffered from gastrointestinal ulcers. The heart of any pharmaceutical company is its research and development function— its laboratories. Unfortunately, SmithKline became fat and happy over Tagamet. It never again came close to creating a similarly profitable new medication, much less creating the pipeline of many different products that is required for sustained success in the pharmaceutical industry. The labs essentially lost the sense of urgency and accountability employed in developing Tagamet. As SmithKline "rested on its laurels," it was leapfrogged by other pharmaceutical companies as it slowly became a second-tier pharmaceutical R&D firm. Subsequent mergers under the names of French, Beckman, and Beecham did little to revive the innovation and drive of its labs. No American pharmaceutical company has ever been bought and sold as many times as the original SmithKline. Finally, in 2001, British pharmaceutical giant Glaxo bought the moribund company, primarily for its veterinary products and over-the-counter personal health-care products, which Glaxo lacked.

A direct link between business failure and failure of a company's culture can be seen in such companies as Arthur Andersen and Coopers & Lybrand of the accounting industry, most of the American steel industry, the airline industry, Kmart, Wang Labs, Columbia/HCA, CSC Index, Polaroid, Montgomery Ward, and Oxford HealthCare. In these and many more companies, management and their boards were ignorant of the direct link between their cultures and their ability to compete in the marketplace. Companies have been pushed to the brink of failure or lost significant market share as a result of underperforming or politicized cultures such as Lucent Technologies, Rite Aid, Motorola, Qwest, Kodak, United Airlines, and Xerox. The highly politicized and fragmented cultures at Motorola and Xerox cost both companies their industry-leading positions around the globe. Xerox went through a period of internecine warfare between 1998 and 2001 that decimated the company and allowed Japanese competitors to take the largest share of the U.S. copier market. At Rite Aid, Columbia/HCA, Enron, Adelphia, and Fannie Mae, financial malfeasance ruined the companies and forced the ouster of their CEOs. We will talk more about these kinds of companies, as they exemplify specific types of cultures. If those companies had invested in building ethical, performance-driven cultures that minimized turf battles, they would have performed up to expectations without the need to cook the books.

CORPORATE CULTURE AND THE BOTTOM LINE

Too few business leaders understand how corporate culture impacts bottom-line performance. Contrary to popular belief, *there is a direct link between corporate culture and financial performance*, as demonstrated by several studies.

A study of more than two hundred publicly traded companies identified as having "high performance cultures" showed that these companies had an increased market value of $35,000 to $80,000 per employee, which was one full standard deviation above those that did not have similar cultures (L. Spencer and C. Morrow, "The Economic Value of Competencies: Measuring the ROI," paper presented at the Third International

Figure 2.1

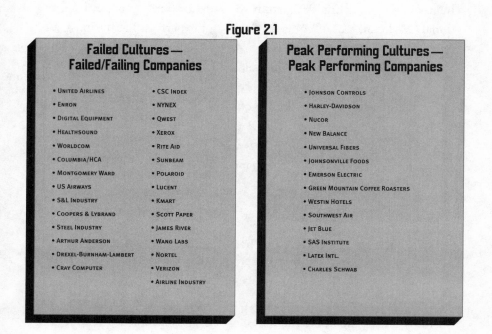

Failed Cultures — Failed/Failing Companies		Peak Performing Cultures — Peak Performing Companies
• UNITED AIRLINES	• CSC INDEX	• JOHNSON CONTROLS
• ENRON	• NYNEX	• HARLEY-DAVIDSON
• DIGITAL EQUIPMENT	• QWEST	• NUCOR
• HEALTHSOUND	• XEROX	• NEW BALANCE
• WORLDCOM	• RITE AID	• UNIVERSAL FIBERS
• COLUMBIA/HCA	• SUNBEAM	• JOHNSONVILLE FOODS
• MONTGOMERY WARD	• POLAROID	• EMERSON ELECTRIC
• US AIRWAYS	• LUCENT	• GREEN MOUNTAIN COFFEE ROASTERS
• S&L INDUSTRY	• KMART	• WESTIN HOTELS
• COOPERS & LYBRAND	• SCOTT PAPER	• SOUTHWEST AIR
• STEEL INDUSTRY	• JAMES RIVER	• JET BLUE
• ARTHUR ANDERSON	• WANG LABS	• SAS INSTITUTE
• DREXEL-BURNHAM-LAMBERT	• NORTEL	• LATEX INTL.
• CRAY COMPUTER	• VERIZON	• CHARLES SCHWAB
	• AIRLINE INDUSTRY	

Conference on Competency-Based Tools and Applications to Drive Organizational Performance, Chicago, Ill., September 1996). In a comparison of sales professionals from companies with high-performing cultures versus sales professionals from other companies, the sales professionals from the high-performing cultures sold an average of $6.7 million versus $3 million from those who were not (J. Hunter and Frank L. Schmidt, "Individual Differences in Output Variability as a Function of Job Complexity," *Journal of Applied Psychology*, February 1990).

The best-known study demonstrating the direct relationship between business culture and financial performance was conducted by John Kotter and James Heskett of Harvard University (*Corporate Culture and Performance*, Free Press, 1992). Over an eleven-year period, Kotter and Heskett found that companies with superior business cultures vastly outperformed those companies that did not:

- Increased revenue average of 682 percent versus 166 percent
- Expanded work forces by 282 percent versus 36 percent
- Stock price growth by 901 percent versus 74 percent
- Net income growth of 756 percent versus 1 percent

In an ongoing benchmarking study by Organization Strategies International (McLean, Va.) of companies with high-performing business cultures compared to companies with average or underperforming cultures, the benchmarked companies (17 of them) averaged 9.8 profitable quarters (out of twelve consecutive quarters) compared to 5.7 profitable quarters for the nonbenchmarked companies (27 of them). Business leaders who reject the importance of business culture as a driver of financial performance may want to compare their own corporate cultures and financial performance to the data from these studies.

THE IMPACT OF CULTURE ON MERGERS AND ACQUISITIONS AND VICE VERSA

Mergers and acquisitions have become important strategic tools for business to expand their market shares or to eliminate a competitor (e.g., Oracle's unfriendly takeover of PeopleSoft). Between 1991 and 2000 there were 19,000 major mergers and acquisitions involving American businesses. Nevertheless, nearly 70 percent of the mergers failed outright or failed to meet their principal business objectives. According to Ernst & Young, a leading financial and accounting consulting firm, the single most prevalent contributor to those failures was the inability or failure of the merging businesses to take into account the different, and sometimes hostile, cultures within the business units being combined. Despite this startling finding, consulting firms, boards, and senior officers of acquiring companies, as well as venture capital firms, ignore the issue of culture and almost never include a culture audit as part of the due diligence evaluation and planning process.

Two significant examples of mergers that went awry, largely around the issue of culture, were the AOL Time Warner merger and the DaimlerChrysler merger. In the AOL Time Warner merger, a new-industry, entrepreneurial, high-tech company from Herndon, Virginia, purchased Time Warner, a more traditional New York–based media and advertising business. There was also a major contrast in management team capabilities and style. AOL had a decidedly less well developed and less traditional management cadre. It also had a more chaotic and less predictable culture typical of Internet businesses. AOL also relied heavily on part-time, hourly workers, many of them college students working in customer-service call centers. High turnover was constant. The rest of the workforce consisted largely of IT professionals. Time Warner had a workforce dominated by full-time employees and a more traditional culture. It had a more diversified business portfolio, including strategic business units in cable television, publishing, and other media. The Time Warner culture was slower, more process-oriented, and more bureaucratic than AOL's. When AOL executives moved to senior corporate positions after the merger, chaos was the order of the day. This did not last long, as Steve Case and his AOL followers and his management team were pushed out of Time Warner. AOL began to function as a business unit within the larger Time Warner business family. Nevertheless, the damage was done: Billions in shareholder value were lost.

COMPONENTS AND CHARACTERISTICS
OF CORPORATE CULTURE

Just as the concept of corporate culture varies so widely in the corporate, academic, and consulting worlds, so do the characteristics and components that comprise corporate culture. Many look at it strictly as the rites and rituals of the company. Most companies have few if any rites or rituals, but they still have cultures. Others see culture as the informal behaviors within the company. But how do we measure or evaluate "informal behaviors" and, more important, change them when required? "Adaptive" and "nonadaptive" as well as "strong" and "weak" are common descriptors assigned to culture, but those terms are vague and resist measurement. More recently, ethical conduct has become the overriding characteristic associated with corporate culture. Certainly, a company's ethical practices are critical to any company's culture, but,

Figure 2.2 Vehicles for Culture Change

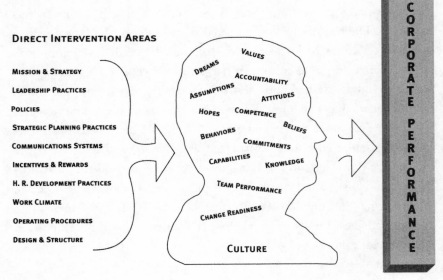

DIRECT INTERVENTION AREAS

MISSION & STRATEGY

LEADERSHIP PRACTICES

POLICIES

STRATEGIC PLANNING PRACTICES

COMMUNICATIONS SYSTEMS

INCENTIVES & REWARDS

H. R. DEVELOPMENT PRACTICES

WORK CLIMATE

OPERATING PROCEDURES

DESIGN & STRUCTURE

DREAMS · VALUES · ACCOUNTABILITY · ASSUMPTIONS · ATTITUDES · HOPES · COMPETENCE · BEHAVIORS · BELIEFS · COMMITMENTS · CAPABILITIES · KNOWLEDGE · TEAM PERFORMANCE · CHANGE READINESS

CULTURE

CORPORATE PERFORMANCE

©1995, copyright revised 2006

again, they are only one dimension. Most companies conduct their business affairs in an ethical manner, but still have cultures that need to be changed, improved, or modified if they are to succeed. *In reality, corporate culture reflects the behaviors, values, dreams, assumptions, hopes, commitments, performance, knowledge, competence, recognition and rewards systems, performance, innovation, and communications that exist within a company.*

In the course of my consulting, I have found that it is best to look at a company's culture through ten different indices that have real meaning to a company's management and workforce. They include:

1. Mission and strategy
2. Leadership and management effectiveness
3. Communications and decision making
4. Organization design and structure
5. Organizational behaviors (including values, ethical conduct, and standards for behavior)
6. Knowledge and competence
7. Business and organizational interventions
8. Innovation and risk taking
9. Performance
10. Change readiness and management

1. MISSION AND STRATEGY

Mission and strategy are critical issues for corporate culture—not just that a mission and a strategy exist but that they are understood, accepted, and acted upon by employees. If the mission and strategy do not directly drive performance, then in reality they do not exist. Far too often, I have seen impressive and articulate mission statements that no one believes. We have all seen them framed and mounted on the walls of every office at a corporate headquarters or field office. In government offices, you see pictures of the currently elected president on the office wall, but in corporate America, the company's mission statement occupies the place of honor. Unfortunately, mission statements are usually drawn up at an officers' retreat and are almost never subject to the input of the larger management team, and certainly not the larger work force. As one Continental pilot told me during the troubled Frank Lorenzo era, "It's their mission, up there on mahogany row. It has nothing to do with the airline that I fly." That statement reflected a total disconnect between management and the rest of the company.

I am frequently asked by senior management teams to help them develop their mission statements by accompanying them to a company retreat or even to draft it for their officer group to approve. In such cases, I always decline. Instead, I propose that there be a companywide mission development process that starts at the top and is rolled down into the company and back up to senior management, thereby gathering in the feedback of middle management and the rank and file. Mission can be a powerful tool for identifying, building, and supporting the culture. Unfortunately, too few companies want to take the time, and I think that many officer groups and boards do not trust the larger workforce to provide its input.

The primary components of a company's corporate mission should consist of:

- Purpose and assumptions (vision)
- Principal business goals
- Corporate identity
- Overriding policies of the company
- Values and standards for behavior

The purpose, assumptions, and business goals of the company may be based on the original vision of its founder—no matter how far in the past that may have been. This would be especially appropriate where the founder or founders are still leading the company, as is the case in today's newer IT and Internet companies. In more established companies, where the founder is no longer on the scene, it is frequently important for the company to get back in touch with the original vision of the founder, especially when the company is in trouble. It may be that the original founder's mission is out of touch with current competitive conditions. In most cases, however, the original mission can help a company with its current struggles and lend clarity to many problems. With the radical change that forces so many companies to dramatically change direction or even industries, the corporate identity is a critical part of the mission. It reflects how the company wants to be recognized in the marketplace as well as within the company.

The mission must clearly state the values and ethical guidelines by which the company will compete in the marketplace. It is a set of self-imposed rules of conduct. Its absence is typical of companies with predatory cultures, which will be discussed in detail in chapter 4. When senior management engages in illegal and unethical conduct, it signals that there is no mission or it is just a framed piece of paper for public relations purposes. When employees engage in behaviors that are contrary to the mission, it means that the mission is not owned by the larger organization. *Corporate mission can be an important tool for changing a company's culture or for returning it to a former lost culture if again required. It helps to define the company to all of its stakeholders, both inside and outside the company.*

Too few leadership teams take into account the relationship between their business strategy and the company's culture. The most obvious example is that the best of business plans can be sabotaged by a culture that cannot support its implementation. A less obvious but equally important factor is whether employees within the company understand the strategy as it affects their work and performance. It does not matter if it is a marketing manager or the switchboard operator; the success of a company's strategy will rely heavily on everyone's understanding of the strategy and their part in helping to achieve it.

2. LEADERSHIP AND MANAGEMENT EFFECTIVENESS

I will discuss, in more depth, the relationship between leadership and corporate culture later in the book. I want to make clear, here, that a leadership team that is ignorant of its corporate culture, specifically, how it affects the implementation of the business's strategy as well as day-to-day operations, is steering a ship without a rudder. Middle managers frequently think that they have a different culture in their part of the organization or within their department or function. Clearly, there are work climate differences between a headquarters and a production plant or a customer service center. In large organizations, there will be subcultures that exhibit differences and unique characteristics compared with the larger corporate culture. Nevertheless, the greater the differences, the more likely there will be trouble for the company. *A major responsibility of management at all levels is to continually build and maintain a common, performance-driven culture with which all employees can identify all around the business. That includes conducting business on behalf of the company in a manner that represents the highest ethical standards and best professional practice.* Unfortunately, most companies today are managed according to the outdated Taylor school of management, which emphasizes top-down decision making, rigid control, and little feedback from the bottom of the company to the top. Ethical standards are too infrequently discussed. In cultures that I call New Age Business Cultures, management emphasizes:

- Innovative thinking and critical feedback from all levels
- Leading versus controlling
- Broad consensus building for moving forward versus Lone Ranger management
- 360° evaluation versus top-down evaluation
- Courageous leadership
- Reasonable risk taking
- Proactive versus reactive stance
- Unassailable ethical conduct

3. *COMMUNICATIONS AND DECISION MAKING*

Communication is a taken-for-granted issue in most companies. There are both formal and informal communications systems in any organization. Companies tend to try to manage formal communications internally through newsletters as well as e-mail, intranets, and formal memos. Most corporate communications to the outside world are now managed by one of the newer bureaucratic functions of the business world—the corporate communications department. It is frequently led by a vice president and manned by a small army of public relations and media "experts," and its news releases and explanations of a company's initiatives or missteps are well planned and highly orchestrated. Management frequently ignores the informal communications within a company that can easily undermine the formal system of communications.

Many in the business world have a tendency to separate the issues of communications and decision making. Nevertheless, the two are linked at the hip, especially within the context of culture. The best decision making will be rendered useless by faulty communications that may be unclear, untimely, or improperly framed and lacking a needed context. When a key decision is communicated to a privileged group at the expense of other interest groups, it has a negative impact on the culture and it says something about the culture itself. This may promote the rise of factions and turf battles. It also creates mistrust while elevating some people above others.

The direction of communications within a company will tell you a lot about its culture. When communications is all top-down, the culture is clearly centralized at the top and reflects a controlling, authoritarian, command-and-control type of culture. The leadership of companies with top-down-only communications is usually blind to changes, potential threats, and opportunities in the marketplace, and the company pays the price. Companies that have a free flow of communications between functions and departments as well as from the bottom up are usually better performing companies.

4. ORGANIZATION DESIGN AND STRUCTURE

Corporate restructuring may be the most common consulting intervention employed in the business world. Typically, consultants look at spans of control and organizational layers and attempt to reduce them. I will deal with the appropriateness of this often-used consulting strategy later in the book, but there is a relationship between culture and organization design.

The Relationship Between Structure and Culture

Early in my consulting career, I was approached by the Contel Corporation, an Atlanta-based telecom and satellite company. Contel wanted me to appraise their company's design and structure to determine how it affected their culture. Led by the visionary Chuck Wohlstetter, Contel management prided itself on having a flat organization and a culture that could respond quickly to market conditions as it systematically took business away from AT&T and, later, the Baby Bells. At first, I was reluctant to take on the engagement, as most organizational consultants at that time would have said that there was no relationship between a company's structure and its culture. Nevertheless, my consulting team and I forged ahead. Indeed, we learned a lot about the company's culture through its rapidly growing and bloated organization design and structure.

The increasing success and expansion of the company was creating a more formal bureaucratic structure that interfered with middle management's ability to respond quickly to marketplace needs. In particular, as the company expanded into thirty states, it grew a more dominant and controlling regulatory function along with burgeoning legal and financial functions. Eventually, these support functions began to replace decision making and action taking by operations managers. Communications and decision making between the top of the company and frontline supervisors and managers were effectively choked off. The alarm was sounded by a middle management engineer who was continually blocked in his attempts to deploy a new "black box technology" in the field. In fact, the more bureaucratic AT&T deployed its own competing technology before Contel. The manager finally parked himself outside the door of CEO Don Weber until he could gain an audience. After a twenty-minute discussion with Weber, the manager was empowered to deploy the new technology. Weber knew he had a bigger problem with the company's design and structure and that it signaled the need for a sea change in Contel's culture, which he set about changing. The burgeoning bureaucratic structure served as a wake-up call to the entire company. Weber saw to it that the company got back in touch with its original culture and vision, which propelled renewed expansion. Contel became the most profitable company in the telecom industry until its purchase by GTE.

A company's design and structure says a lot about its culture and it has a strong impact on a culture's performance that goes well beyond size, headcount, spans of control, and layers. Organization design can hinder or aid the exchange of information, communications, resources, and ideas within the company. It can help a company interface effectively and speedily with its customers and suppliers or it can drive those customers away through incessant roadblocks. Organization design and structure have everything to do with "goodness of fit" with markets, mission and strategy, and culture and operations. It can be rigid and hierarchical or responsive and flexible. It can either support people's efforts or it can block their best efforts.

A dramatic example was seen at Lotus Development. Under founder and CEO Mitch Kapor, Lotus was a company with few rules and fewer internal bureaucratic barriers. People could access talent, resources, and innovative ideas from anywhere in the company almost at will. Kapor decided that he was no longer suited to running a company, and he replaced himself with Jim Manzi of McKinsey in 1986. Lotus's informal and relatively unstructured environment was foreign to Manzi, and he set about changing it. It was not long before Lotus was broken into silos, which was a popular move in the 1980s and early 1990s in large corporate America (this silo effect nearly ruined IBM before the Gerstner era). Everything was now controlled from the top down, and there was little interaction and sharing between the silos created under Manzi. The result was devastating to a company that was known for rapidly delivering the most innovative of software products of its day. Now their pipeline was slow, and products were delivered long after projected deadlines. In particular, their new spreadsheet, known as Lotus 123, was more than a year late in reaching the marketplace. This allowed Lotus's competitors an opportunity to introduce their own products before Lotus. It not only cost the company customers, it cost them the confidence of their investors. Eventually, key talent and technology was sold to IBM as the company structure hamstrung its once innovative culture and prevented it from introducing new products in a timely manner.

In presenting these two examples from Lotus and Contel, I run the risk of reinforcing another misconception and overused failed initiative in the marketplace—that restructuring will solve culture problems. No concept could be farther from the truth: Rearranging an organization chart does very little to change an underperforming culture. A company's structure does reflect problems with the culture.

5. ORGANIZATIONAL BEHAVIORS AND CONDUCT

The organizational behaviors and conduct of people within an organization are at the core of business culture. This includes ethical conduct. Whether they be behaviors of excess as exhibited by Dennis Kozlowski at Tyco, excessive careerism of aspiring middle managers, or rude and self-important behavior by secretaries and receptionists over the phone, they all offer telling vignettes of a company's culture. Behaviors constitute a realm of business performance that managers and leaders just do not want to deal with. They act as if people's behaviors do not exist and are of no consequence to the business.

Positive and productive behaviors serve as the glue that holds an organization together while supporting the performance of the business through:

- Effective team building and collaboration versus the need to play Lone Ranger
- Responsiveness to customers and suppliers versus treating the customers as a bother
- Candor and openness versus covert behavior
- Taking responsibility for mistakes as well as successes versus denying responsibility and casting blame onto others
- Allowing and learning from failures versus zero tolerance for failures

■ Engaging in best professional practice versus doing what is easy and convenient

■ Valuing team victories over individual successes versus the need to be a hero and indispensable savior

■ Openness to change and new learning versus slavish commitment to the tried, true, and familiar

■ Taking appropriate risks versus playing it safe

■ Ethical conduct that serves all of the stakeholders versus self-serving ethical standards for a select few within the business

As I look at these standards for conduct, I immediately think back to elementary school days where these standards for conduct were taught, starting in the first grade. We also act in accordance with these standards, more or less, in our personal lives. Unfortunately, too many of us have worked within companies where these behaviors occur only sporadically. Corporate Darwinism seems to take over once one enters the workplace. The released tapes of Enron energy traders laughing at "grandmas" having to pay higher electric bills as a result of their greed and malfeasance is a chilling example of a different mind-set in that particular workplace. The same behavior was exhibited by BP energy traders in 2005. Companies also impose strong pressure on employees, especially new employees, to conform to a strict code of behavioral rules:

"Always wear a white shirt and tie" or "Never wear a dress shirt and tie" (in many of today's high-tech companies).

"Don't bypass the boss if you have a problem with the boss."

"New people should be seen, not heard."

This includes innovative thinking. In many organizations, innovative ideas and new approaches are expected to come from the top, not percolate from the bottom up. Regardless of the industry, innovative thinking and "pushing the envelope" are critical to a company's success and very survival.

6. KNOWLEDGE AND COMPETENCE

Originally, "in-house training" was just that—developing skills to be more efficient and to promote a safe work environment. Today, many large corporations are well known for their learning centers and corporate universities. GE pioneered the concept in 1956 with its leadership and management school. Leading learning centers have been developed at IBM, 3M, McDonald's (Hamburger U.), and Motorola University (a fully accredited university), to name just a few. Even smaller companies feel the need to have their own learning centers, despite the high cost. A major strength and weakness of these centers is that they focus almost exclusively on developing new leaders.

Nevertheless, it seems that these learning centers do little to build competence into the culture. I wonder how many companies and institutions remain in business when confronted by the overwhelming lack of knowledge and competence exhibited by their employees, managers, and executives. I say this not just as a consultant, but as a consumer and as an observer of our business and government organizations as well as a participant in society. Despite the explosion of information and constant availability of new tools for accessing it, people within work environments seem to be less informed and less competent than previously, whether it be the switchboard receptionist, executive assistant, division head, department manager, customer service representative, or the most senior executive. They all seem to have tunnel vision focused just on the narrow limitations of their assigned roles.

On the surface, knowledge and competence seem to be separate issues, and they are treated as such by organizations. Peter Senge, author of *The Fifth Discipline,* made popular the idea that organizations need to continually engage themselves in education and learning. *Unfortunately, there seems to be a great void between acquiring knowledge and actually applying it to drive performance within organizations.* While educational experiences for management do not necessarily have to provide immediate rewards, education and learning seem to fail as drivers for downstream competence in most companies today.

The *customer service department* in most companies is either not empowered to solve problems for customers or simply does not have the education, training, and resources to get the job done. They lack competence. Neither do they rate high in the eyes of management or the larger business organization. As a retired director of customer service (and former operations director) of a major utility company noted, "Customer service departments are not usually staffed with the best and brightest of the company, nor are they given the resources or authority to get the job done, properly, as is the case in operations."

The same seems to apply to *administrative staff*. A company makes a major statement about its organizational competence just by the manner in which secretaries and receptionists carry out the normal responsibilities of their roles. Too often, their conduct hinders rather than supports the daily affairs of a business. These key people are relied upon as the grease that keeps a company's daily operations and communications operating smoothly. Nevertheless, they seem to work with blinders on, not knowing who the key people are in other departments or how to access resources when they are most needed. My own firm once approached a major professional services firm to invite a partner to speak at a forum we were sponsoring. At first, no one on the switchboard had him listed. We were then connected to the firm's managing partner. His secretary had heard of him but was not sure what office he was in. She promised to get back to us, but never did.

As part of an organization performance audit that I conducted for a professional services firm, I asked employees several questions about administrative competence and effectiveness, as that was a concern for the principals of the firm. Administrative and secretarial staff scored low on such evaluative statements as:

"Effectively solve problems on their own"

"Easily access resources and help from other areas of the firm"

"Meet deadlines on time with a minimum of excuses"

"Complete work with a high degree of accuracy the first time"

"Put the needs of managers, consultants, and the larger organization above their own"

"Are consistently competent and knowledgeable about most
administrative responsibilities"

"Deal with outside callers in a professional and helpful manner."

As one partner in the firm described it, "They are their own informal
union, with their own work rules and subculture. I'm sure we have lost
clients because of the way they interact with people from the outside.
No one dares cross them." This is an organization that is held hostage by
its administrative staff, but it may also be that the firm's partners do not
value their administrative staff and do not set clear expectations, empower them to be good service providers, or reward them for being good
service professionals. This firm's administrative staff is not atypical.

MIDDLE MANAGEMENT has been squeezed out of many businesses, leaving an overworked cadre of professionals who usually take most of the
blame for corporate missteps and problems. After a downsizing, the
"lucky" middle managers who remain are expected to pick up the slack
from their laid-off coworkers. Managers are expected to be the eyes
and ears of the business as well as serve as the implementers of corporate strategy. Middle managers are expected to be the top problem
solvers, traffic cops, masters of communication as well as the motiva-
tors, developers, and evaluators of staff. Because so much is expected of
them, their ranks swell again from the need to specialize their roles—
only to be downsized again. Developing and retaining competent middle managers may be impossible within the traditional business culture.

LEADERS are expected to exhibit strong competencies in the areas of
strategy formulation, organization building, people motivation, and influence building while setting an ethical compass for everyone within
the business. They must also be decisive decision makers, effective com-
municators, and exceptional action takers (execution). Nevertheless, in
more than two decades of coaching CEOs and their executive teams, I
have found that almost all CEOs and their senior executives have fallen
short in these critical areas of leadership competence. When I was
asked to present my findings to a group of CEOs and COOs by an association, I asked them to identify the most important single competency that they were expected to exhibit in their roles. Overwhelmingly,

the most prevalent answer was to deliver positive financial returns to the shareholders. Is this the competency expected of CEOs or of money fund managers? I am convinced that all other areas of organizational competence will suffer until the people on top change their priorities about their own set of required competencies.

7. BUSINESS AND ORGANIZATIONAL INTERVENTIONS

A business organization must engage in effective problem solving and make the right course corrections at the right time. Management must demonstrate the ability to correctly appraise internal needs and problems in a many areas, with as little bias as possible, and then implement the most effective course correction. Whether we are talking about a Fortune 500 company or a smaller business, the company's needs and problems are complex and do not readily lend themselves to quick fixes or to applying a solution developed in some other company. Unfortunately, business leaders and their managers seem to fall back on restructuring or business process reengineering (BPR) or the latest IT improvement to solve almost any problem they face. With the issue of a failing corporate culture, very few organizations recognize the need, while failing, to employ a highly individualized approach that is appropriate to their unique business and the competitive conditions that are challenging the company.

8. INNOVATION AND RISK TAKING

Innovation and risk taking are becoming scarce commodities in the business world. The trend toward ever larger corporations has created increased needs for control by management as well as rigid and complex bureaucracies. These and other forces have diminished innovation in the corporate world and make it more difficult, and threatening, to engage in risk taking. When Ed Zander took over Motorola, he moved the company's R&D capabilities to downtown Chicago, away from the corporate headquarters campus in Schaumburg, Illinois, to minimize the bureaucratic and political roadblocks to creating new technology. People also feel constrained from providing critical feedback to their colleagues and supervisors within larger and more authoritarian work environments. Opportunities for innovation and risk taking must be a major component of any culture. Motorola is working to rebuild a culture of innovation, risk taking, and, most especially, collegiality throughout the organization.

9. PERFORMANCE

In recent years, companies have put a premium on measuring the performance of people. All kinds of "people accountability" measures have been instituted within companies, with 360-degree evaluation being the most prominent of these processes. *Unfortunately, companies rarely understand how to translate people performance into organizational performance, which ultimately drives bottom-line performance. The missing link is culture.* Companies can better understand and build performance-driven organizations by understanding how their cultures drive—or obstruct—bottom-line performance. This includes being able to measure the performance of a company's culture. In 2005, I made an informal inquiry into twenty-two companies that were in the news for various competitive issues that were impacting each company. I asked if they had undertaken a corporate culture audit or planning process within the past two years. Two said that they had, but when I delved further into the nature of the audit-planning process, I found one was clearly an operational and cost reduction study and the other was not at all systematic, consisting of a "few focus groups being conducted around the company."

10. CHANGE READINESS AND MANAGEMENT

A common characteristic among failed and failing companies is their inability to accept and prepare for change—*change readiness.* In the age of radical change, it is no longer possible to sustain high-performing businesses with traditional business planning or the usual operational efficiency improvements. Cost cutting has been pushed to the extreme as a "strategy." *The best performing companies are able to create change in the marketplace.* Companies that compete effectively are able to understand changing business conditions around them while responding in ways that allow them to take advantage of the changed business climate. This is called change management. In this age of radically changed business conditions, all others can only expect to hold on until they fail or are saved from failure through an acquisition.

FIVE KEY REQUIREMENTS FOR EFFECTIVE CHANGE MANAGEMENT:

CLOSE THE GAP BETWEEN BUSINESS PLANNING AND ORGANIZATION PLANNING

No business plan will succeed unless an effective organization is in place to support and implement it. This includes a committed, well-trained, and competent workforce; effective communications; competent management that can think outside the box while motivating workers to perform effectively, and leadership that is visionary and ethical. It requires the right culture to implement the business plan.

CREATE A CORPORATE CULTURE THAT EMBRACES CHANGE

Change-ready cultures contribute the most to business performance. These New Age business cultures are flexible, open, searching, and innovative, and are loosely structured rather than rigidly hierarchical. Change-ready cultures encourage reasonable risk taking and critical feedback, but they are also supportive of good efforts regardless of their outcome, whether successful or unsuccessful. Change-ready cultures are able to respond to changing market conditions more quickly compared to more traditional cultures that are slow, resistant to change, suspicious of innovative ideas, and dependent upon top-down decision making before taking action. Leaders of New Age cultures are secure enough to let the organization make decisions and move forward absent their own approval. (New Age business cultures will be discussed in more detail in chapter 6.)

IDENTIFY ALTERNATIVE CRITICAL SUCCESS FACTORS FOR MANAGERS

The traditional manager who gives orders, supervises people, and evaluates performance by herself is a thing of the past. These command-and-control managers do not successfully motivate employees or earn their trust and commitment. According to Jim Coblin, vice president of human resources at industry-leading Nucor Corporation, successful managers in that company provide resources to their employees while trusting them to make decisions and take quick action to solve problems on their own. "People here don't worry about bosses thinking for them. Any new supervisor who feels that they have to be in control at Nucor will find that their shift's productivity will not measure up and that, after six months, they will have been fired by their own employees."

New Age managers must:

■ Become students of the company's culture and be able to nurture the culture as it exists in their area of the company

■ Disperse problem solving and decision making through worker empowerment

■ Provide resources for employees to be successful, not roadblocks

■ Share rewards and risks among the workforce

■ Give honest, direct, and factual feedback whenever needed

■ Look beyond the usual threats and opportunities scenario to become change managers, not just operational managers

KEEP INNOVATIVE PEOPLE AND THEIR IDEAS AT HOME

A major debate has arisen in the media and among politicians over outsourcing and offshoring of jobs. The debate started over the outsourcing of jobs to companies that would provide the same services but without the overhead to the company. This was accomplished by reducing pay to their own workers while reducing or eliminating many benefits. The debate became noisier with the offshoring to Asia of production jobs, then call center jobs, and now high-level knowledge-based positions, especially in technology and accounting. This was highlighted in 2005 when Microsoft moved eighty software architect jobs to Asia to save money. These positions represented the apex of the innovation and knowledge-based pyramid. Does a Fortune 50 company like Microsoft really need the money so badly that they have to send these positions overseas?

American companies are under pressure to cut overhead as they compete in an increasingly global marketplace. Yet, corporate boards need to ask if cost savings should be the ultimate, and in many cases, the only criterion for moving talent overseas. Are there consequences to massive offshoring, and if so, what are they? Will there be any impact on developing, recruiting, and retaining committed American talent? Will American business become a backwater for the creation of new products, business processes, and markets? What are the implications for business culture? Will it become irrelevant?

These questions may be answered by what is happening in India and, especially, in China. India develops some of the very best technology talent in the world, but it is severely limited in how many promising students it can admit to its universities because there are so few of them. China has had even fewer institutions of higher learning in which to train its youth. Beginning in the late 1970s, both countries began to encourage their youth to seek higher education in America, and American universities were happy to increase their enrollments with English-speaking students from Asia. Many stayed to be employed in American companies, especially the Indian students who have a command of English, while others returned to their homelands to work in Chinese and Indian divisions of American companies. That career path is starting to change. India and China are developing world-class companies of their own that can compete very effectively with their American counterparts. As a result, they are recruiting their native sons away from American companies.

In addition, technology and knowledge have become commodities that know no boundaries, especially in China, where international copyright and patent protections are often ignored. The bottom line is that American companies have to decide if they want to be the training ground for future top talent that will compete against them in foreign companies or whether they want to protect their investment and future success by creating cultures that will retain top knowledge workers and the intellectual capital they create. *American companies have to create cultures that keep innovative people and their ideas at home.* More important, American companies have to send a signal that it is all right to develop one's education, talent, and expertise, as they will be valued by American companies and will guarantee them a career that will not be off-shored.

CONTINUALLY AUDIT THE ORGANIZATION

Continuous auditing and monitoring of the company's culture and overall organizational effectiveness is obligatory. In the age of radical change, a company must always know if its culture is appropriate for the new competitive challenges confronting the company. Without understanding the strengths and weaknesses of its own internal culture, a company's leadership will be ill-prepared to meet unforseen challenges from the marketplace.

3

BEWARE THE FADS
AND FIX-ITS

Fad Surfing: the practice of riding the crest of the latest
management panacea and then paddling out again just in time
to ride the next one; always absorbing for management and
lucrative for consultants; frequently disastrous for
organizations.

—Eileen Shapiro, Author of *Fad Surfing in the Board Room*

The age of radical change will not be known only for its tumultuous
business conditions, technology explosion, overnight creation of entirely
new industries, or the rise of highly interdependent and competitive
global markets across almost every industry. It will also be known for its
failures, its scandals, and its "charlatans." After a year at the helm of a
high-tech manufacturing company, a CEO once lamented that he could
never really find the outside consulting help or the internal corporate resources he needed to effect real change within his company. "We are in
the same place as we were three years ago. There are a lot of charlatans
out there who want to sell nothing more than the usual fads and fix-its
with new labels attached to them." Unfortunately, in an effort to gain a
competitive edge in the age of radical change, most corporations have
relied on a host of charlatans for failed remedies, magic bullets, and fads
that rarely deal with the core issue—*changing a company's culture.*

The last fifteen years have brought a parade of "solutions" including business process reengineering (BPR), downsizing and rightsizing, various total quality management (TQM) initiatives, zero-based budgeting, overhead budget management (OBM), go-for-growth strategies, and the usual, failed business planning exercises. In recent years, businesses have resorted to a number of financial manipulations and outright looting that have destroyed shareholder value and, in many cases, entire companies. I was recently asked whether corporate culture caused many of these problems. My answer was an unequivocal yes. In the wake of such scandals, companies now resort to the latest silver bullets—crisis management and marketing spin.

PUBLIC RELATIONS AND MARKETING TO MASK MORE FUNDAMENTAL BUSINESS PROBLEMS

Crisis management firms are the latest entrants to the business consulting world; their aim is to help companies to clean up their tarnished images after deceiving shareholders or consumers. Their stock-in-trade is to counter negative revelations about a company with spin, image building, focus groups, and renewed advertising of reliable, well-known products. Through internal company memos, it was revealed that pharmaceutical giant Merck had known for years that its arthritis drug Vioxx posed a threat for sudden cardiac failure in certain patients. The company's initial response was to have then-CEO Raymond Gilmartin stick out his chin and indignantly assert that Merck had done nothing wrong and it would fight every legal claim and win. When it lost its first court case, Merck countered with advertising and PR statements heralding its research to find cures for childhood diseases and its expanded offers of drug discounts for seniors. At one time, Merck sat atop the pharmaceutical industry (also once known as the *ethical* drug industry) with an unmatched pipeline of groundbreaking drugs and never a hint of false representations about its products. The problems Merck now faces are reminiscent of another scandal at the long-ago failed pharmaceutical giant, A. H. Robbins Pharmaceuticals of Richmond, Virginia. Robbins was forced out of business because of problems with its Dalkon Shield birth control device.

In the wake of accounting scandals at insurance giant AIG (American International Group), the firm placed the blame on its legendary chairman Hank Greenberg and pushed him out. At the same time, AIG flooded the media with ads for its various financial products, implying that AIG was a safe place for investors. What these companies all lacked were ethically focused, performance-driven cultures. The need to market and sell displaced the need for ethical conduct and best professional practice to support performance.

Marketing has also been used as a tool to mask more fundamental problems in a company. Based on the track records of Jill Barad, former CEO at Mattel, and Carly Fiorina, former Hewlett-Packard CEO, marketing executives may not be the best choices for leading an entire organization and certainly not a company's culture. At struggling Mattel, former marketing executive Barad's approach was to market the company out of its difficulties, never recognizing that the culture at the toy maker was as out of date as were many of its products. The company was nearly bankrupted under her watch. Fiorina brought a strong marketing mind to HP and little else, which I will discuss later in this chapter.

BUSINESS PROCESS REENGINEERING

If ever there was a hoax imposed upon the business world, it was business process reengineering (BPR). BPR was originally developed by former Deloitte and Touche IT consultant Thomas Davenport (later a professor of information sciences at the University of Texas). BPR was the product of information systems modeling, and was intended for use within the realm of information systems only. Davenport has repeatedly asserted that he never intended BPR to be an all-encompassing tool for business and organization improvement as it was widely sold by James Champy and Michael Hammer. Eventually, BPR became a boon to the consulting industry, as almost every major consulting firm and thousands of small consulting shops and individual consultants took on BPR as the ultimate consulting intervention for transforming the business organization. Champy and Hammer were able to sell BPR to Computer Sciences Corporation, then enlisted their financial backing in starting CSC Index, a firm dedicated to providing BPR consulting to the business world. Eventually, BPR was recognized as a highly flawed product. Rather than improve business processes, it monopolized the attention of company management by seriously disrupting normal business functioning, harming existing corporate cultures, reducing—not improving—productivity, while alienating workers and management. Some of the failings of BPR included:

- It was overly complex, requiring BPR "specialists for almost every aspect of the business";
- BPR was not "workforce friendly," as most workforces were ill-prepared to master the BPR processes;
- As an information systems model, it was improperly extended for use to broader areas of business planning and functioning; and
- Rather than reducing bureaucracy, it required an increased IT bureaucracy that was dedicated to monitoring and maintaining BPR processes everywhere within the company.

As more consulting firms sold BPR to their clients, each firm had to give it its own stamp, and BPR eventually became many things rather than one identifiable discipline. BPR rarely improved a company's culture; instead, it imposed significant stress on the company's culture and, many times, destroyed it.

The only measurable outcome of BRP was massive layoffs, which Champy and Hammer pointed to as a major cost-saving benefit of BPR. How that is different from the usual downsizing that companies regularly undertake remains a mystery. Eventually companies had to staff up again as BPR flushed key people and capabilities from the companies. As the division general manager of a medical parts manufacturing company noted, "Now that everyone is gone as a result of the BPR, no one is around to actually produce the product, get it to the customer, and provide after-sales support. We were stripped bare by BPR."

In their efforts to catch up to Wal-Mart, management at Kmart brought in one of the major consulting firms to reduce costs and improve its business processes using BPR. They stipulated, however, that the consulting firm could not reduce the company's head count by more than one percent as a result of the BPR process. After nearly eighteen months and $2 million in consulting fees, both Kmart management and the consulting firm gave up. The net overhead reduction never came close to approaching the goal for cost reductions, and the chief information officer noted that "business processes were more muddled than ever before."

U.S. West was determined to undertake BPR by themselves without the support of an outside firm. After nearly three years, the telecom giant gave up on BPR, noting the conflicting organization structures that had emerged, and decreased customer satisfaction seen through increased consumer complaints to the Public Utility Commission.

CSC Index itself recognized that BPR had its problems and that it was having an unintended, negative influence on the cultures of many of their client companies. They set about trying to acquire a corporate culture consulting firm to put back together the culture of their client companies after their BPR consulting. Eight years after their start-up, parent company Computer Sciences Corporation closed down CSC Index due to increasing criticisms and mounting lawsuits. The most troubling aspect of BPR was that the corporate world was convinced that it was the right thing to do, given that so many other companies were using BPR. I call this the lemming effect, which is too widespread in the business world.

THE MAGIC WAND OF RESTRUCTURING

Without a doubt, restructuring (including downsizing and rightsizing) has been the most commonly utilized business intervention in the corporate world. Hardly a company of any size has not been subjected to continual restructuring and downsizing activities. Restructuring has been used as a remedy for a host of corporate problems, including failed business strategy, poor financial performance, ineffective or incompetent management, underperforming corporate culture, and failed responses to change. Restructuring is also used to rein in bloated bureaucracies and, most often, is implemented to compensate for previously failed or incomplete restructuring efforts. According to the American Management Association, 65 percent of companies that downsize repeat the process within a year. In 1993, Arthur D. Little partner Robert Tomasko published a study of 1,000 companies that undertook the downsizing and restructuring process and found that:

■ Ninety percent expected to reduce expenses, but fewer than half succeeded.

■ More than half expected to reduce bureaucracy, but only 15 percent claimed success.

■ Seventy-five percent sought productivity improvements, but only 22 percent reached their goal.

Arthur D. Little repeated the study in 2000 and reported almost identical results. In another study, conducted between 2000 and 2002, Organization Strategies surveyed 236 companies and found that:

■ Managers in 184 of the companies felt that the restructuring effort did not justify the cost.

■ One hundred sixty-three of the companies had to repeat the restructuring within two years.

■ The restructuring effort was perceived as having a negative impact on the culture in 178 of the companies.

Restructuring can help clarify overlapping management structures and reduce unnecessary layers of a bureaucracy. However, restructuring and downsizing will not:

■ Improve a failing corporate culture,

■ Enhance faulty decision making,

■ Improve employee performance and commitment,

■ Correct a flawed business strategy,

■ Compensate for failed leadership, or

■ Satisfy disaffected customers.

Downsizing and restructuring will make companies smaller, and may even reduce the scope of some of their problems, but they have not yet proven that they will improve the performance of a company. *I truly believe that most CEOs resort to downsizing and restructuring in a desperate attempt to show investors that they are in control and have a definitive answer to problems within the company.* Wall Street likes downsizing though it has little effect on improving the performance of companies. In reality, such efforts reveal that CEOs are lacking the know-how and leverage to effect real change within their companies, especially when the need is to change the culture.

THE FAILED PROMISE OF BUSINESS PLANNING

In the course of my career, I have seen countless companies undertake formal business planning efforts only to have them fail. After restructuring and downsizing, business planning has been the most preferred and failed tool of the consulting industry. Consulting giant McKinsey made its reputation on business planning, as did a host of other firms. Nevertheless, Michael Porter has commented that "the criticism of the strategic planning was well deserved as strategic planning in most companies has not contributed to strategic thinking" ("Corporate Strategy, the State of Strategic Thinking," *Economist*, May 1987). Henry Gomer of Harvard has noted that "formal planning does not provide early warning or make an organization more sensitive to environmental change" (in H. Mintzberg, *The Rise and Fall of Strategic Planning,* Free Press, 1994). Business planning was born in the 1960s and early 1970s when business leaders were confronted with a dwindling supply of domestic natural resources that were required to sustain industrial production. The 1973 oil crisis created a new sense of urgency in corporations and spurred the overnight growth of business planning as a major business tool. Originally, business planning was a by-product of World War II supply and logistics planning to support the war effort. Business planning was later devised to help companies plan around anticipated scarcities of resources while attempting to identify and control overseas resources.

Unfortunately, companies tried to enlarge the business planning process to do more than it could appropriately accomplish. Internal strategic-planning departments and outside consultants were expected to apply the business planning process to create a "futures" scenario for their own businesses, taking into account internal technology and people requirements as well as competitor behavior and marketplace uncertainties. Business planning has largely failed for the following reasons:

- Traditional business planning assumes that the marketplace is rational and predictable. The current climate of radically changing business conditions leaves no time for business plans to be enacted and renders the traditional business plan obsolete before the ink has dried on the report.

- Business planning is seen as a fixed activity that has a start and finish, yielding an end product. To be effective and relevant, it must be a dynamic, ongoing process. Change management and strategic management have started to replace business planning, as they entail an ongoing process with no particular end point or end product, while emphasizing internal capabilities and resources of the company as sources of creating change.

- Business planning almost always excludes middle management from the planning process, and middle managers are usually in the best position to recognize internal operational obstacles that will confound any new business plan.

- Business planning fails to take into account a company's culture and whether that culture can support the new business plan or whether (as in most cases), it will be an obstacle to the plan's fulfillment. (J. Want and W. DuSualt, *The President*, American Management Association, 1990).

Companies that maintain dynamic, innovative, open cultures are in a better position to respond rapidly and effectively to radically changing market conditions. In many cases, these New Age business cultures, as I like to call them, create the change and leave it up to their competitors to play catch-up. Increasingly industry leaders such as Nucor and Johnson & Johnson spurn torturous planning practices and rely on their cultures to identify and respond to opportunities in the ever-changing marketplace with new products and services. They create change in the marketplace by forcing their competitors to play by their rules—usually forcing them to engage in business planning exercises.

THE URGE TO MERGE

As we've seen in chapter 2, business combinations have become a blunt instrument for achieving almost any business objective or for overcoming any business obstacle. Like restructuring and downsizing, mergers seem to be an obligatory tool for CEOs who want to show they are in charge. In a study of fifty-eight mergers between 2000 and 2004, Organization Strategies found that only four of the postmerger teams focused their attention on culture as a recognizable key component of the postmerger integration process.

As we've seen, the AOL Time Warner merger tried to blend two starkly different cultures and leadership styles. New York City–based Time Warner was a company steeped in tradition, with its roots going back nearly a century. Its culture was characterized by process, careful planning, and a more traditional and centralized leadership style. In contrast, with its headquarters built in the middle of a former cow pasture in rural northern Virginia, AOL was a true New Age company that brought the Internet into wide use. It was led by people with strong marketing and sales backgrounds from such companies as Pepsico and Century 21 Real Estate. Much of its workforce consisted of part-time college student "techies." Its culture was anything but process oriented; it was chaotic. Its customer-service function was at the center of its operations and was a persistent problem that eventually led to massive customer defections. At first, the goal was for Time Warner to purchase AOL, but AOL's artificially inflated stock value made it more feasible for AOL to purchase Time Warner. There were immediate problems when Steve Case and his AOL management team brought their thin portfolio of corporate experience and chaotic

Figure 3.1 Failed Mergers from Failed Cultures

- HEWLETT-PACKARD 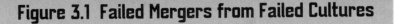 COMPAQ
- AOL ⇨ TIME WARNER
- MORGAN STANLEY ⇨ DEAN WITTER
- SBC ⇨ PACIFIC TELESIS
- QUAKER OATS ⇨ SNAPPLE
- WORLDCOM ⇨ MCI
- DAIMLER ⇨ CHRYSLER
- COMPAQ ⇨ DEC
- GE ⇨ KIDDER PEABODY
- NOVELL ⇨ WORD PERFECT
- FIRST UNION ⇨ CORE STATES
- SMITHKLINE ⇨ FRENCH/BECKMAN/BEECHAM
- AT&T ⇨ NCR
- DEUTSCHE BANK ⇨ BANKERS TRUST
- TARGET ⇨ MARSHALL FIELDS

leadership style to the top echelons of the newly combined company. Friction between Case and Time Warner's Jerry Levin could not be hidden. Case and his AOL comrades were ousted, and the highly anticipated synergy between the two companies was little more than another failed business plan. When it was learned that AOL had misstated its financials for the period prior to the merger, the new AOL Time Warner stock plummeted.

Culture immediately killed the Quaker Oats–Snapple merger. Quaker Oats, in business for nearly one hundred fifty years, had a slow, bureaucratic culture. It saw its consumer products as commodities. Snapple was a much newer, fast-growing company that penetrated the marketplace through aggressive marketing, especially to younger consumers. Snapple sales slowed to a halt as many of its managers left.

Quaker Oats then tried to spin off Snapple, and the two were eventually purchased by Pepsico.

The GE–Kidder Peabody merger failed on the basis of very different approaches to ethical conduct in the marketplace. GE is a company that has avoided scandal and competed in an ethical manner in the marketplace. Shortly after taking over Kidder Peabody, GE discovered fraudulent trading practices and a predatory culture within the Paine Webber unit that led to federal scrutiny and sanctions. Less than five years after the purchase, GE divested the investment bank. This was a vivid example of GE's failure to investigate and understand the culture of a very different business.

A good example of how corporate culture is so misunderstood within the context of a merger was seen in the failed acquisition of Compaq by Hewlett-Packard. At the time of the announced merger, Susan Bowick, then executive vice president of human resources for Hewlett-Packard, proclaimed in the media that "the cultures of the two companies are so similar that it will not pose an obstacle to the merger." In reality, two high-tech companies could not have had more different cultures. HP had a company history and culture that were steeped in an almost mystical tradition, cutting-edge R&D, a meritorious culture, and a distinctive psychological contract emphasizing mutual commitment between the workforce and management. Compaq, on the other hand, was not known for developing technology but for acquiring it, as it did with its acquisition of Digital Equipment. In fact, Compaq was known to have a highly politicized culture that continually resorted to large-scale layoffs when the markets went down, only to ramp up to meet increasing demand. It was a veritable roller coaster at Compaq, as one former human resource manager noted. That merger was widely regarded as a failure in that it harmed, rather than improved, shareholder value in the company; HP's overall market share was only slightly enhanced by the acquisition, and only in servers. It is true that when Fiorina took over HP, the company was in a slump, but it did not help the company when she thumbed her nose at the decades-old HP culture. Instead of relying on the company's strengths, including its renowned reputation for innovation, Fiorina resorted to conventional downsizing, deal making (mergers), and new marketing and advertising initiatives, which was her calling card based on her years of experience in the Bell telecom environment. Economies of scale have been the oft-proposed justification for entering into a merger, but I do not think that anyone really believes this mantra anymore.

CORPORATE CULTURE AS THE LATEST FAD?

In one way, it is refreshing to have the recent wave of corporate scandals and business failures laid at the altar of neglected and failed culture by the media. Nevertheless, my fear is that the issue of culture will become just the latest fad that makes for good headlines in the business media only to be forgotten in time and put back on the shelf. Corporate culture building remains the most underutilized resource for improving business performance. Business as usual will no longer suffice when the very existence of the business organization, as we know it, is at risk. The best-devised PR plan will not prevent customers, shareholders, and employees from seeing the true nature of a company's failed culture. The very best industrial engineers know that there is a limit to how many new efficiencies can be squeezed out of the production process when operations are held back by an underperforming culture. Nor will cost reductions and restructuring compensate for an unresponsive, bureaucratic culture. The best-crafted business plan will fail when it relies on a culture that has lost its commitment to the business. As seen in Figure 3.2, corporate culture building is one of the more strategic tools to be utilized within a company, but like any unused tool, it will become rusty over time when not properly cared for.

Corporate leaders and their managers do not have to become "masters of their corporate cultures," Jerry Egar, consultant and former professor at Chicago's Loyola University, noted, and I rather doubt that any corporate culture can be "mastered." However, managers and leaders can become effective developers, managers, and stewards of the culture. This is best accomplished by understanding how culture building fits into the array of business strategies and interventions.

Figure 3.2 Strategic versus Tactical Interventions

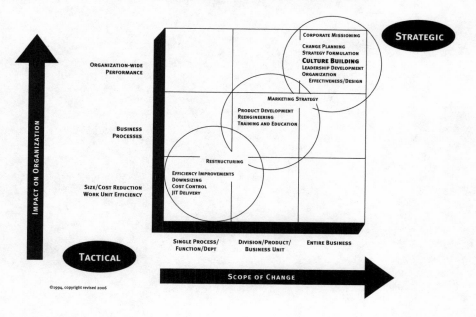

Employees at all levels of an organization must take ownership of the culture and not assume that there is nothing they can do about it. A company's culture is made of people, and the people within that organization can and must take responsibility for their culture. The alternative is that corporate culture will be just the latest fad leading to widespread business failure.

PART II THE HIERARCHY OF CORPORATE CULTURES

4

FAILED AND FAILING CULTURES

Leave my factories but take away my people and soon grass will grow on my factory floors. Take my factories, but leave my people and soon, we will have new and better plants.

—Andrew Carnegie

Too often corporate culture is dismissed as vague, undefined, and disconnected from day-to-day business affairs and as having little impact on the bottom line. Companies may pay it lip service, but too frequently it is treated as a transitory issue to be filed away and forgotten. These people fail to understand that their company's culture influences virtually all of their daily activities and overall performance. *Unfortunately, most management and leadership teams think that their company's culture is invisible to the marketplace when it is invisible only to them.* In reality, a company's culture is quite apparent to customers, investors, suppliers, and other stakeholders in the business.

In recent years the effects of underperforming and failed cultures have even been the subject of numerous media headlines. Microsoft has garnered headlines in *Business Week* and other business journals for its predatory culture, which drives talent to its competition. Fannie Mae's financial malfeasance, and the subsequent firing of its CEO, Harold Raines, were heralded in every major media outlet. The McWane Company has been the subject of intense scrutiny for fouling the environment while exposing its workers to dangerous work conditions. In the government sector, "culture problems" at the CIA and FBI have been daily fare in the media, as have the bureaucratic failings of the FEMA "culture" and those of its parent, the Department of Homeland Security.

In 2005, Verizon's stock lost 26 percent of its value, a loss traceable in large part to its ponderous culture and unresponsive management. These problems go ignored by Ivan Seidenberg, who favors continued acquisitions and the adoption of new technology for which the marketplace is not always willing to pay. At the time of Bell Atlantic's acquisition of NYNEX (forming today's Verizon), it was not widely known that NYNEX (one of the original Baby Bells) was technically bankrupt and had gone hat in hand to Bell Atlantic to be rescued. Unfortunately, NYNEX management eventually gained control of the new company as Bell Atlantic management arranged to be paid off en route to retirement. No company can afford to let this happen, as companies with underperforming and indifferent cultures drive customers to competitors and undermine investor confidence.

THE HIERARCHY OF BUSINESS CULTURES

Over the years, I have used the hierarchy of business cultures to demystify the subject of corporate culture and to put it into a business context for client companies. The hierarchy of business cultures serves several purposes:

- It helps overcome vague and incomplete notions about the subject—it makes culture real;
- It differentiates among different cultures found in different companies and industries;
- It connects the subject of culture to our own companies and our own work; and

■ It allows us to make a direct connection between business culture and business performance.

I have found that seven distinct types of cultures exist within the business world, each with its own set of characteristics and qualities. From the poorest performing to the best performing, they are:

1. Predatory cultures
2. Frozen cultures
3. Chaotic cultures
4. Political cultures
5. Bureaucratic cultures
6. Service cultures
7. New Age cultures

The first five types fall into a category that may be characterized as underperforming, failing, or failed. These I also call "cultures of shame," as there is no good business reason for these five types to be maintained; they rarely satisfy anyone's expectations. The Service and New Age cultures I classify as high-performing cultures in that they meet or exceed expectations of most of the stakeholders of the business. New Age cultures are the most responsive to change or best able to create change in the marketplace.

In this chapter, I will focus on the five types of underperforming cultures. (I will discuss service and New Age cultures in chapter 6.) Please note at once that organizations may exhibit characteristics of more than one type of culture. They are called subcultures or backup cultures. This is normal, especially in highly complex, diversified organizations and in holding companies, such as United Technologies and General Electric, where very different strategic business units from different industries come under a single corporate banner. In many cases, these are not different cultures so much as they are different work environments. *Even where it is appropriate to have subcultures, there should be a dominant, overriding corporate culture by which the entire business should be recognized.*

Figure 4.1 Hierarchy of Corporate Cultures

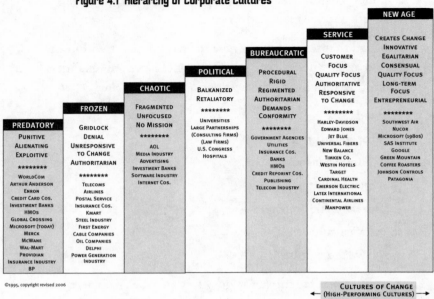

PREDATORY	FROZEN	CHAOTIC	POLITICAL	BUREAUCRATIC	SERVICE	NEW AGE
						CREATES CHANGE
						INNOVATIVE
					SERVICE	EGALITARIAN
				BUREAUCRATIC	CUSTOMER	CONSENSUAL
					FOCUS	QUALITY FOCUS
			POLITICAL	PROCEDURAL	QUALITY FOCUS	LONG-TERM
				RIGID	AUTHORITATIVE	FOCUS
		CHAOTIC	BALKANIZED	REGIMENTED	RESPONSIVE	ENTREPRENEURIAL
			RETALIATORY	AUTHORITARIAN	TO CHANGE	
	FROZEN	FRAGMENTED		DEMANDS		★★★★★★★★
		UNFOCUSED	★★★★★★★★	CONFORMITY	★★★★★★★★	SOUTHWEST AIR
PREDATORY	GRIDLOCK	NO MISSION	UNIVERSITIES		HARLEY-DAVIDSON	NUCOR
PUNITIVE	DENIAL		LARGE PARTNERSHIPS	★★★★★★★★	EDWARD JONES	MICROSOFT (1980s)
ALIENATING	UNRESPONSIVE	★★★★★★★★	(CONSULTING FIRMS)	GOVERNMENT AGENCIES	JET BLUE	SAS INSTITUTE
EXPLOITIVE	TO CHANGE	AOL	(LAW FIRMS)	UTILITIES	UNIVERSAL FIBERS	GOOGLE
	AUTHORITARIAN	MEDIA INDUSTRY	U.S. CONGRESS	INSURANCE COS.	NEW BALANCE	GREEN MOUNTAIN
★★★★★★★★		ADVERTISING	HOSPITALS	BANKS	TIMKEN CO.	COFFEE ROASTERS
WORLDCOM	★★★★★★★★	INVESTMENT BANKS		HMOS	WESTIN HOTELS	JOHNSON CONTROLS
ARTHUR ANDERSON	TELECOMS	SOFTWARE INDUSTRY		CREDIT REPORINT COS.	TARGET	PATAGONIA
ENRON	AIRLINES	INTERNET COS.		PUBLISHING	CARDINAL HEALTH	
CREDIT CARD COS.	POSTAL SERVICE			TELECOM INDUSTRY	EMERSON ELECTRIC	
INVESTMENT BANKS	INSURANCE COS.				LATEX INTERNATIONAL	
HMOS	KMART				CONTINENTAL AIRLINES	
GLOBAL CROSSING	STEEL INDUSTRY				MANPOWER	
MICROSOFT (TODAY)	FIRST ENERGY					
MERCK	CABLE COMPANIES					
MCWANE	OIL COMPANIES					
WAL-MART	DELPHI					
PROVIDIAN	POWER GENERATION					
INSURANCE INDUSTRY	INDUSTRY					
BP						

©1995, copyright revised 2006

CULTURES OF CHANGE
◄── (HIGH-PERFORMING CULTURES) ──►

PREDATORY CULTURES

Companies with predatory cultures have gained significant media attention in the past five years through indictments of numerous corporate
leaders, the forced restatement of false financial reports, predatory employment practices, consumer and investor fraud, and even destruction
of the environment. Predatory cultures fail to have a motivating and
strategic vision that binds the company together. They have few rules of
conduct, guiding principles, common values, or common rites and rituals. If a formal corporate mission statement exists, it is usually false and
ignored. Neither do predatory cultures engender employee commitment, customer satisfaction, or investor confidence. Predatory cultures
are blind to the stakeholders of the business and are not able to anticipate the consequences of their actions. As a result, they are rarely able to
change from the inside and are inevitably forced to change by outside
forces such as extreme shareholder pressure, regulatory scrutiny, or legal
action. The preferred stakeholders of a company having a predatory cul-

ture are usually a small, privileged group comprising a special group of investors or a select cadre of senior officers. Predatory cultures are known for their retaliation against those who do not agree with them, exploitation of broader stakeholder groups, as well as a punitive and alienating work environment. Communication within predatory cultures is also closed and secretive and is usually top-down. There is little tolerance for bottom-up communication and feedback. As a result, there is reduced worker initiative and commitment compared to other cultures. Predatory cultures also have a higher turnover rate among workers and management.

Figure 4.2

PREDATORY

PUNITIVE
ALIENATING
EXPLOITIVE

****

WORLDCOM
ARTHUR ANDERSON
ENRON
CREDIT CARD COS.
INVESTMENT BANKS
HMOs
GLOBAL CROSSING
MICROSOFT (TODAY)
MERCK
MCWANE
WAL-MART
PROVIDIAN
INSURANCE INDUSTRY
BP

The Polaroid Corporation is an example of a company that has been taken over by a predatory culture. Once an admired business known for new technology that helped to create a new industry, Polaroid went into bankruptcy in 2004. At the same time, senior managers approved pay increases and bonuses for themselves and gave lucrative consulting contracts to many executives who were downsized out of the company. Employees, shareholders, and customers were left out in the cold. Today the very existence of the company remains in doubt. The preferred stakeholders that have taken control of Polaroid may be looking to further enrich themselves through a potential acquisition.

Many times, predatory cultures are born of the tremendous success of once high-performing, innovative cultures. Examples include Microsoft, Enron, Arthur Andersen, AIG, Marsh McLennan, and Merck, to name a few. Enron was not just one of the fastest-growing companies to reach the Fortune 10 level, it was considered a preferred employer. The consequences of its now infamous culture made it anything but a preferred employer, supplier, or investment vehicle. Arthur Andersen was a pioneer firm in the accounting world as it did more to lead the accounting sector into full service IT and general management consulting than any of the other major accounting firms. It was also a great place to work. Nevertheless, the lawless actions of a number of its audit partners destroyed the firm's century-old reputation for excellence and integrity and wiped out all of the partners.

For many years, Merck sat atop the global pharmaceutical industry. Its unending pipeline of new drugs was unmatched by any other pharmaceutical company. Its culture was devoted to exceptional research, ethical practices, and steadfast commitment to its employees. The Vioxx scandal revealed a company that had lost its way by putting sales and marketing targets ahead of best professional practices. It has been reported that internal documents showed the company knew that Vioxx posed a clear risk to some patients. In the wake of the scandal, the company was forced to undertake painful and unprecedented layoffs.

In the 1980s, Microsoft would have been described as having a New Age culture by any standard. It was a magnet for top technology talent and an economic engine for the entire country as well as the computing and software sectors. It practically invented the personal computing industry and made many of its rank-and-file employees millionaires. Something happened to the company in the 1990s, when its leadership began to focus obsessively on monopolizing the software and computing sectors as well as the Internet. Eventually, Microsoft came under severe criticism from competitors for predatory pricing and monopolistic practices. In 2004, it was forced to agree to federal court strictures to limit its monopolistic behavior in the marketplace (and critics say Microsoft seems to not be abiding by those guidelines). In 2005 and again in 2006 the European Commission imposed its own penalties and restrictions on Microsoft for predatory practices. More revealing has been the number of defections by some of its top talent to competitors, leaving an internal culture that has been described as bureaucratic, oppressive, and slow-moving—in short, a culture lacking the innovation and creativity that distinguished it originally. In addition, morale has sagged, and employee stock options have been described as "valueless." Microsoft employees are said to be especially unhappy because of pay cuts and reductions in benefits while company profits continue to soar (*Business Week,* September 26, 2005). Microsoft is a company that has turned to the "dark side" while becoming a predatory culture.

Wal-Mart has a culture that divides the country into those who hate it and those who love it. Many love it for its low prices. So do many of its workers, who would not be able to find employment in their rural communities were it not for Wal-Mart. But others bitterly attack Wal-Mart's culture and policies. Much of its predatory behavior comes from its poor pay and even poorer benefits for its employees. The retail industry is not known for high wages, and Wal-Mart consistently pays its employees below industry averages. The company has also been the subject of EEOC actions for discriminatory promotion practices against its female employees. In addition, Wal-Mart has been under attack for hiring illegal aliens to build stores around the country while paying them less than the minimum wage.

Wal-Mart has long been criticized for its strategy of opening stores near small-town market centers all across America, thus putting them out of business. Suppliers who want to do business with Wal-Mart are forced to price their products so close to cost that they cannot make a fair profit. Zeiss Labs, USA, is an example. This manufacturer of high-quality eyeglass lenses has been forced to cut the price of its high-end products for Wal-Mart optical departments to the point of making very little profit. If a supplier responds by ceasing to do business with Wal-Mart, it will lose even more market share in the United States—market share that it helped Wal-Mart to build. Now, Wal-Mart also buys heavily from suppliers in China to cut its costs, driving many of its former American suppliers out of business. American grocery chains are under severe attack by Wal-Mart, even in markets where Wal-Mart has no presence. Wal-Mart prevents unionization and severely restricts employee wages and benefits. Wal-Mart thereby drives down the price of goods and especially labor, making it harder for grocery stores to compete. The reduced labor costs are critical to Wal-Mart's success but are poison to grocery store chains, which have had decades-old relationships with unions. The key to Wal-Mart management's strategy is to transfer risk and costs to employees and suppliers. This profile represents a company with a predatory culture.

Companies with predatory cultures have high turnover rates (unless employees are held captive by restricted work opportunities). There is little team building, and innovation is nearly nonexistent. There are few standards for behavior or ethical conduct, as was seen at Enron. New employees have trouble fitting into predatory cultures and typically have short tenures with such companies. Frequently, management thinks that it can drive performance by pitting workers against each other. In reality, performance is stymied and people feel exploited. Coopers and Lybrand was such a company. Known as the Cadillac of the Big Eight accounting and management consulting firms, its internal culture was marked by incessant infighting among partners and consultants at almost all levels of the firm and by excessive careerism by ambitious managers and consultants. It was said that "you went to work at C&L each day with a football helmet on." Eventually, its internal battles made it vulnerable to a takeover by the much smaller Price Waterhouse, which bought out more than two-thirds of the C&L partners to get them to leave the newly formed Price Waterhouse Coopers.

Predatory cultures also exhibit themselves in subtler ways, especially in dealing with customers in the retail marketplace. Branch Banking and Trust of Winston-Salem, North Carolina, is an example. This fast-growing regional bank has set its sights on developing a presence in the Washington, D.C., marketplace, which is known for its highly educated workforce as well as for a climate of strong customer service that is rarely matched in other parts of the country. Nevertheless, BB&T's practices seem to run counter to these characteristics. Unlike other banks, it will not increase the daily limit for customer withdrawals, and it cherry-picks customers for loans. More critically, their bank operations personnel are poorly trained and supervised and paid below-market wages. The result is frequent staff turnover and numerous problems in back office and branch operations. When BB&T management is given critical feedback by customers on such issues, they have been known to retaliate by closing the customers' accounts.

It seems that the financial services sector is most prone to generating predatory cultures. In each of the last three decades of the twentieth century and again in the early years of the twenty-first century, investment banking, brokerage, commercial banking, and insurance firms were convicted of various forms of fraud. Many Wall Street firms have been convicted of fraudulent practices or fined by the Securities and Exchange Commission or state regulatory commission. For various reasons, including mergers, former Wall Street giants such as Prudential Securities, Drexel Burnham Lambert, Kidder Peabody, E. F. Hutton, and Shearson Lehman are now just fading memories. A number of smaller firms disappeared, too. One would think that companies like Morgan Stanley and Merrill Lynch would learn from history, but some of their employees continue to betray investor confidence, as seen in the repeated legal actions, fines, and regulatory sanctions that are imposed on them. I do believe that the leaders of these companies think that they are just too big to fail. More important, they fail to understand the cultures of their own companies—and know much less about how to develop and manage these cultures.

FROZEN CULTURES

Frozen cultures are paralyzed by gridlock and denial. These cultures have an aversion to innovation and risk taking. The aversion to risk taking starts at the top and is imposed on the entire organization by management. New ideas rarely see the light of day, and an employee's stepping outside the chain of command is not tolerated: Going around a boss can quickly end a career. Companies with frozen cultures are always behind the change curve and must play catch-up to industry leaders. Frozen cultures have obsolete missions and strategies, and frequently the strategy is nonexistent or out of touch with marketplace changes. Leadership is usually authoritarian— not authoritative—and must be the source of all decision making. The outcome is that management is working with blinders on, having excluded other sources of information and insight that might help lift the company. This negates the value of frontline

Figure 4.3

FROZEN

GRIDLOCK
DENIAL
UNRESPONSIVE
TO CHANGE
AUTHORITARIAN

****

TELECOMS
AIRLINES
POSTAL SERVICE
INSURANCE COS.
KMART
STEEL INDUSTRY
FIRST ENERGY
CABLE COMPANIES
OIL COMPANIES
DELPHI
POWER GENERATION
INDUSTRY

management as well as rank-and-file workers, who usually see the problems at the market level long before middle and senior management. Kmart in the 1980s and 1990s was an excellent example of a company with a frozen culture.

[CASE STUDY]

Kmart—A Fortune 50 Company Frozen in Time

The first time I drove up to the Kmart headquarters in Troy, Michigan, I was somewhat amazed by the size of the headquarters building. It seemed to go on forever, and I spent more than ten minutes driving around to find the right entrance. In total, there were twenty-three entrances to the building, labeled with letters from the alphabet. I was later told that the local police department deployed a special traffic detail twice daily to redirect traffic in and around Troy during the morning and afternoon rush hours. Kmart's nearly 12,000 employees arrived and left at virtually the same time each day. When I tried to walk around the building from one meeting to another, I was either late or never found the meeting room. It was like finding your way around an aircraft carrier, especially with its split floors. Outside vendors always required a map to find their way, and I found myself relying on guides whenever I could. On one occasion, even my guide became lost. The cavernous main entrance was decked with banners proclaiming 2000—the number of stores to be opened by the year 2000. That was the focus of Kmart's new business strategy—growth. The only problem was that Kmart was already overextended. The company was losing customers and market share to Wal-Mart and an up-and-coming discount chain—Target—that was known for its upscale merchandise and shopping environment.

To my surprise, I was invited to Kmart by the chief information officer—not the CEO, COO, or the chief human resources officer, as was usually the case. The company had just completed a BPR engagement under the direction of the CIO and an outside consulting firm, and it had failed to meet its objectives. What had been revealed was a frozen culture that was just not responding to customer needs and a middle-management cadre that moved in lockstep to orders from above. Founded in 1899 as Kresge, the company invented the discount shopping experience. During the Depression, it specialized in selling items that cost five or ten cents (the five-and-dime store), and after World War II, it was a mainstay for growing American families, but by the 1980s, it was losing market share to Wal-Mart and Target. In 1990, Kresge changed its name to Kmart and expanded its stores. Ironically, many of the principles that made Wal-Mart number one were actually copied from Kmart, as Kmart was increasingly out of touch with its original mission and changes in the marketplace. In every measured category, Kmart lagged behind its competitors, especially in the all-important return per square foot of retail space.

Its growing list of problems included: supply chain breakdowns, universally poor service in its stores, a high turnover rate among store associates (usually leaving for Wal-Mart and Target), unmarked merchandise (at one point measured at nearly 50 percent in one spot survey), and an increasing exodus of store managers and middle management. As conditions deteriorated, decision making was increasingly directed from above, with middle management rarely involved. A group of middle managers reported that they were unable to send feedback and ideas to higher management ranks. Similar stories came from store managers. Communications were effectively blocked by a highly rigid and layered bureaucracy. CEO Joe Antonini himself controlled hiring at the corporate headquarters (along with all of his normal duties), and anyone being hired with a salary exceeding $35,000 had to be personally approved by him, often after he had interviewed the candidate. Kmart was a Fortune 50 company with more than 250,000 employees.

Adding to Kmart's problems was an ongoing battle between two of its top officers who reported to Antonini. The officer in charge of U.S. operations and the officer in charge of overseas operations (principally Canada and Europe) were engaged in perpetual all-out warfare. When they did communicate with each other, it was at the upper end of the decibel range, according to one executive. Neither would attend Antonini's executive staff meetings if the other was there. In addition, the rest of senior management knew that it could not act without Antonini's approval. Other, more basic problems put Kmart at a competitive disadvantage, most especially its supply-chain management, which was based on a twenty-year-old distribution system. The CIO had struggled to implement a computerized just-in-time system that was more in line with Wal-Mart's system, but he failed to gain approval from Antonini and the executive team. The two warring executives could not agree on one system, as each wanted a system of his own design, one giving him direct control over merchandise and supply-chain decisions. At the same time, Wal-Mart's system was fully computerized and required no management approval. It was also directly linked to its largest supplier, Procter & Gamble. Furthermore, Kmart's once-famed associates training program was outdated. Just as revealing was the company's failure to utilize new information technology. An example was Kmart's failure to put in place e-mail communications until January 2001.

The CIO was correctly convinced that the culture was at the heart of many of Kmart's problems. Unfortunately, and not surprisingly, our combined efforts to introduce culture building at the company failed. Like all of his predecessors, Joe Antonini had risen through the ranks to the top of the company. He was also the first Kmart CEO to be dismissed. (Financial losses were mounting, with no end to the red ink in sight.) The goal of opening 2000 stores by the year 2000 was shelved. One successor, the first to be hired from outside the company, focused on better-quality merchandise, but did little to improve distribution and customer service. Another tried to improve customer service in the stores. His efforts were short-lived, as he was dismissed for signing off on false financial statements. After seven straight years of billion-dollar losses, Kmart was finally forced into bankruptcy protection in 2002, and that forced the closing of more than a third of its stores. Eventually, the company was forced into a merger with Sears. Today, it has the same number of stores as Target, approximately 1,500, but its gross revenue ($19 billion) is less than half of Target's ($47 billion), and its profits ($1.6 billion) are just a third of Target's ($3.6 billion). By retail industry standards, this means that Kmart is still failing.

Kmart is an example of a company with a frozen culture. It was blind to major new competitive changes in the marketplace and ignorant of emerging new technologies required to keep pace with its competition, and it ignored the negative impact of its own culture on its ability to survive. Kmart was still functioning as it did in the 1950s when it was Kresge.

Frozen cultures can also frustrate the best intentions of very capable CEOs. A prime example is the failed marriage between George Fisher and Kodak. After a successful tenure at Motorola, Fisher jumped to Kodak. At first, it seemed to be a great fit. Kodak was losing significant market share to its Japanese competitors, and its own products were being shut out of the Japanese market. Kodak also knew that it had to migrate its technology to new digital imaging. Fisher was clearly the right choice, given his experience in expanding Motorola's presence in Asia. Fisher also had a first-rate technology mind. Unfortunately, Kodak's culture proved to be more than a match for Fisher. At Motorola, he sat atop a highly politicized, some would say fractious, corporate culture but one that was known for developing and producing innovative, new technology. Kodak, on the other hand, had a century-old frozen culture that was slow-moving and resistant to new ideas, new management practices, and new technology. In addition, the average Kodak manager had put in nearly thirty years working in the company. Management was slow to accept new ideas.

Nearly every initiative that Fisher tried to implement was met with resistance by Kodak's culture and by challenges from the marketplace. Eventually, he resorted to massive downsizing, that continues today (10,000 layoffs in 2005 after 20,000 previously), and the sale of major business units, including its Eastman Chemical company. These kinds of conventional initiatives could have been implemented by any CEO or turnaround specialist, and were a waste of Fisher's capabilities as a first-rate leader of technology companies. After just six years, Fisher retired from Kodak at age fifty-eight, with many of the company's goals unrealized.

Entire industries have exhibited frozen cultures. We need only look at the American auto manufacturing industry, the U.S. domestic airline industry (some would say the worldwide airline industry), the paper manufacturing industry, the telecom industry, and the domestic steel industry. All seem to be gripped by fear and inaction, which are reflected by each industry's poor financial performance and its contraction. In the airline industry, each of the legacy carriers has adopted bankruptcy as a business strategy. That is, they have resorted to the bankruptcy courts for resolving their labor and operational issues.

Interestingly, in the 1970s, the airline industry unanimously supported deregulation, but they have, in effect, reregulated themselves today through bankruptcy. None of them have considered reinventing their cultures as one way of making their companies profitable and efficient. Instead, they are wedded to a centuries-old, adversarial relationship with their workforces. Neither have the unions tried to develop new partnership with the companies through which everyone might benefit.

Nevertheless, each of those failing industries does have one or two companies that have demonstrated an ability to prosper while running against industry trends. In steel, it has been Nucor (which will be highlighted in chapter 6). In the airline industry, Southwest Air continues to prosper while the remainder of the industry is mired in bankruptcy.

In the auto industry, Toyota remains the most profitable car manufacturer and is on the verge of becoming the world's largest auto maker as GM continues to downsize and lose money. Toyota and Honda have even increased their workforces in America.

Figure 4.4

CHAOTIC
FRAGMENTED **UNFOCUSED** **NO MISSION**
****
AOL **MEDIA INDUSTRY** **ADVERTISING** **INVESTMENT BANKS** **SOFTWARE INDUSTRY** **INTERNET COS.**

CHAOTIC CULTURES

More than once, I have been asked why I place chaotic cultures above frozen cultures in the Hierarchy of Business Cultures. I do so because chaotic cultures can be potentially more productive than frozen cultures. At least, there is significantly more activity in companies with chaotic cultures than frozen cultures, even if much of it is misdirected. At times, someone is able to harness that activity and chaos to direct it in one direction to support performance. People who work within chaotic cultures are frequently receptive to that leadership. *Nevertheless, chaotic cultures continue to be inconsistent if not perpetually weak performers.*

Chaotic cultures are fragmented and unfocused. They rarely have a focused mission or strategy that can be sustained in the marketplace. It is not uncommon for these companies to have a series of failed business plans. Much of the chaos comes from chaotic leadership that is indecisive, inconsistent, and ineffective. As a result, companies with chaotic cultures have difficulty responding to the competition in a sustained and coherent manner. They also make for poor employers, given the unpredictable and chaotic nature of the work environment. As a result, innovation and risk taking are inconsistent. Team building is ineffective. Workers are easily alienated and may be reluctant to make long-term commitments to the company. This, in turn, creates high employee turnover. Policies and operational practices are also constantly changing along with new organizational charts. Chaotic cultures are famous for introducing new flow charts and reorganization schemes based on the flawed notion that the proper organization structure will resolve their problems. As a consequence, reporting relationships, communications, and decision making are in a state of constant turmoil. The marketplace is quick to recognize this chaos, and customers will choose other, more reliable suppliers who are more stable and predictable.

Industries known for chaotic cultures include media and advertising, software, Internet service providers, and investment banking. Almost everyone has a favorite complaint about service and reliability from ISPs. There is often no consistency between what is sold and what is delivered. Nor is there any consistency between two different customer support representatives or two billing representatives within the same company. Part of the problem is that the leaders of ISPs have long felt that younger, part-time support workers satisfy a younger consumer (upon which the Internet market was built) while restraining personnel costs. Nor do ISPs invest in sufficient training beyond rudimentary technical skills. Professionalism, competence, and accountability are sorely lacking.

Many newly emerging companies (the development side of the change curve) also exhibit characteristics of chaotic cultures. These newer companies have to create stable operations and business practices and, most important, make culture building a key component of them. Unfortunately, too many leaders of these companies ignore their newly emerging cultures, which remain chaotic. Google is such a company having a chaotic culture. While it has become a magnet for top talent, and has become an overnight force in its industry, its internal operations and support functions are incredibly chaotic. This chaos is beginning to restrict Google's ability to create and deploy new technology.

AOL has always been known for its chaotic culture. Much of this is attributed to its emphasis on maintaining a temporary workforce for customer support. To control costs, AOL's management has relied heavily on an hourly, part-time workforce of younger customer service and technical support workers. They also have offshored much of the workforce to Asia to further control costs. As a result, these frontline workers who interface directly with customers have little commitment to serving them and have a high turnover rate. It has been reported that the turnover rate among AOL's customer service and technical support workforce exceeds 60 percent each year. Training and supervision of new technical and customer support staff are limited to a few hours, and consist mainly of describing the services that can and cannot be provided—do's and don'ts. There is no sense of culture building. Expectations for best professional practice and satisfying customer needs are nonexistent. There is no accountability to the customer.

Many of AOL's problems can be attributed to the company's original leadership, which had little organizational management experience but was steeped in sales experience. It is no accident that AOL has averaged a net loss of more than four million customers for each of the past five years. The AOL Time Warner board had little patience with Steve Case and associates and jettisoned them. Rarely has there been a less favorable fit between cultures as between Time Warner, with a steady and predictable culture and leadership, and AOL, with its chaotic culture and unproven leadership and management. Rather than change its culture to improve service, AOL decided to not charge for its Internet service reducing the need to improve its customer service.

The former investment bank Shearson Lehman was born with a chaotic culture that directly contributed to its failure. Created to compete with Merrill Lynch, Shearson Lehman was already an uneasy amalgamation of a number of different Wall Street firms when it purchased the prestigious but deeply troubled E. F. Hutton. The partners from the various merged firms were more committed to their previous companies, prerogatives, and turf than to the new and enlarged enterprise. Shearson Lehman was the second-largest Wall Street firm, but it existed for less than a decade because no leader was able to forge it into one firm.

Companies with chaotic cultures face a special challenge when they seek investment capital, as they have difficulty gaining committed investors. Companies with chaotic cultures usually have shorter life spans unless they are in a homogeneous marketplace where most of their competitors have similar cultures. That does not protect them from being purchased for their strategic assets by a larger, more diversified company.

[CASE STUDY]

Coopers & Lybrand—The Cadillac of the Big Eight Firms That Became a Studebaker

Arthur Andersen may have been the largest of the original Big Eight audit and consulting firms (based primarily on its IT consulting), but Coopers & Lybrand was widely considered the "Cadillac of the original Big Eight" for its innovative consulting and exceptional depth of talent in audit and accounting and especially for its general management and strategy consulting. No other Big Eight firm approached C&L in the consulting realm. It also managed to avoid much of the scandal that plagued some of its competitors, such as Peat Marwick (later KMPG) and Arthur Andersen, in the savings and loan crisis. Like its brethren, it started as an accounting and auditing firm and later recognized the need and benefits of providing management consulting to its existing audit clients. By the 1980s, it had grown into the second largest consulting firm in the world, after McKinsey.

The rationale for developing management consulting capabilities was that management consulting services could be sold to existing audit clients (one-stop shopping) and would grow at a time when accounting and audit services were limited by the number of client companies a firm served. As a result of the wave of mergers in the 1970s, many major companies were disappearing, draining the pool of potential clients. By 1980, growth on the audit and accounting sides of the Big Eight firms slowed to just 2–3 percent per year, while management consulting was growing at a double-digit rate. At Coopers & Lybrand, the management consulting business was growing at an annual 18 percent rate.

Nevertheless, there were problems in paradise. The rules of the accounting profession restricted professionals who were not certified public accountants from holding the "partner" title, a restriction that many of the firms upheld. In addition, the rules of the profession limited the ownership positions and voting rights of those who were not CPAs. As a result, many of the firms awarded titles such as "principal" to employees but limited voting rights and stock ownership in the firms to the management consulting "partners" and principals. At Coopers & Lybrand, those who ran management consulting practices were permitted to hold the title of partner as the firm reestablished itself as a professional service partnership and not just as an audit and accounting firm. Nevertheless, many if not most of the audit partners expressed great resentment toward the management consulting partners (MCs). Audit partners continued to "own" the clients. That meant that before a management consulting partner could approach an audit client, the audit partner had to give his or her permission. Many of the partners did not freely offer their permission, and that excluded C&L MCs from bidding on many contracts against other firms. As a result, MCs started marketing to companies that were not C&L audit clients. In other cases, the audit partners exercised control over how much could be billed for a management consulting engagement. Outside the Big Eight, fees billed for management consultants were considerably higher than fees charged for accountants and auditors. As a result, management consultants and partners were paid less than their counterparts in other management consulting firms.

I worked at C&L early in my career and I was surprised to find that on more than one occasion my proposals had to be approved not just by my group MC partner, but also by the audit partner of the client firm. In one case, my proposed fees for a rather sizable organization audit were slashed by the audit partner. In fact, they were reduced to the point where neither the client nor I felt that the consulting could be properly delivered, and the firm and I lost the engagement.

Internal competition for promotion was fierce and was heavily based on billable hours and on one's ability to sell the business. Managers and consultants competed fiercely to get themselves onto en-gagements and to be able to join a sales team. I remember clearly, when I first reported to C&L in New York, that one of my "colleague" consultants in the Organization Effectiveness Practice kept avoiding me and was difficult to engage in conversation. After a couple weeks, I in-vited Chris to join me for lunch so that we could become better ac-quainted and maybe find ways to collaborate on an engagement, but he refused my invitation. I finally confronted him as to why he was so hostile and not "collegial." I'll never forget his response. "You don't get it, if Frank"—our immediate boss—"is not promoted to partner and has to leave the firm, then one of us will replace him, and I don't want to give you a leg up on me." For my entire tenure at C&L, Chris and I never worked together on any engagements. Many other aspects of daily life within the firm were subject to a chaotic culture. This included contin-ual struggles to gain administrative support, authorizations, and re-sources, especially when one needed a proposal to be typed by a deadline. Each day was like a ride on a merry-go-round.

Turnover was especially high among C&L's senior consultants and managers. The firm's organization chart was constantly changing, with practices being moved out from under one partner and put with an-other. The names of the practices and the services they provided were also in constant flux. To make matters worse, the firm had recruited, some years earlier, a number of partners from Booz Allen Hamilton, which had a reputation for a chaotic and brutal culture of its own, and those partners brought much of that culture with them. C&L's leader-ship structure was also quite decentralized compared to the other Big Eight firms and other management consulting firms. The senior partner for the worldwide consulting unit did not have authority over managing partners in various cities, as did his counterparts in the other firms. In fact, he was also paid considerably less. Each partner pretty much ruled his region like a feudal baron while he showed little allegiance to the senior partner. As a result, it was hard to go to market as a firm any-where in the country. Local city partners controlled local engagements even though they did not have the full range of consulting capabilities as did the larger cities of New York and Chicago. When I was invited to a New York partners meeting to make a presentation and had the rare op-portunity to sit through part of the meeting, I was astounded to find that

most of the audit partners sat on one side of the room and the MC partners on the other side. That said a lot about the partners' culture. The
discussion was acrimonious and was also split down the aisle, with the
audit and MC partners squared off against each other. I was happy to
give my presentation and leave.

Despite its many advantages, Coopers & Lybrand's chaotic culture
continually put it at a distinct disadvantage in its industry. Eventually,
as the industry began to consolidate, C&L was involved in a merger, but
unlike the other firms it was purchased by much smaller Price Waterhouse, the second smallest of the Big Eight firms. Price Waterhouse
had solved its own in-house problems between partners and was able
to function as a unified firm when going to market. When it purchased
C&L, it expelled nearly two-thirds of the C&L partners in an effort to
eliminate the chaos for which C&L was known.

POLITICAL CULTURES

Even the most positive cultures have an element of politics, but in companies with political cultures the internal jockeying for influence, turf,
and career advancement dominates the company's agenda. The organization never equals the sum of its parts. Political cultures can also be
mistaken for predatory or chaotic cultures. But political cultures differ
in that they do have implicit rules on how politics is played, while setting some limits on the disorganization and dissension. The final consequences are very different, too, as companies with political cultures
remain in business longer; companies with chaotic cultures have a
greater tendency to fail or be taken over by a competitor. It is not unusual for political cultures to devolve into chaotic cultures, a descent
that can signal the end of the company.

Companies with political cultures have a reasonably well-defined mission and strategy, but they are inconsistently implemented. As the politics
start to spin out of control, a strong leader may help the company refocus
on its mission and strategy to overcome the excessive politics. Too often,

reorganizing and restructuring are implemented to overcome an excessive political culture, but this approach almost always fails. Culture building is the most reliable tool for transforming a political culture into a more cohesive and unified culture. *The key to change in the company is either the progenitor of the politics or the product of it.* To get to the top of a company with a political culture, one must be the true "political animal," which makes it more difficult for such a leader to change the culture. Initiative and commitment is usually centered around the most recent set of political factors. Many times, employee loyalties to a particular manager or to a component of the company (department, function, or division) take strong precedence over commitment to the company. Strong loyalty to the boss also provides employees some degree of protection from the constant politicking, at least until the boss is promoted or removed. Retaliation is a frequently used tool when an employee or department

Figure 4.5

POLITICAL

**BALKANIZED
RETALIATORY**

****

**UNIVERSITIES
LARGE PARTNERSHIPS
(CONSULTING FIRMS)
(LAW FIRMS)
U.S. CONGRESS
HOSPITALS**

does not show sufficient loyalty to the boss. Not surprisingly, companies with a political culture are highly balkanized or fractionalized. This in turn has a negative impact on operations and administrative support services. As a result, the company is an inconsistent performer because it has trouble keeping politics away from suppliers and customers.

Partnerships, large professional service firms, and universities are examples of organizations that are prone to having political cultures. Nevertheless, political cultures can be found in companies of almost any size or type. The ultimate political organization is the U.S. Congress, where politics is the true business product or outcome. That should be the defining factor for highly political business organizations. Politics should not be the end product.

[CASE STUDY]

The Motorola Corporation—An Industry Leader Brought Down
by Political Warfare

Motorola was a company with a highly politicized culture, and in many ways, its founder, Paul Galvin, intended it to be that way. Its initial product was the wireless radio linking police cars with their dispatchers. With this product, Motorola ushered in the wireless communications age. World War II created a great demand for the company's products by the military, which accelerated its growth and diversification and made it a leading source of new communications devices. It eventually expanded into such far-flung markets as television manufacturing and semiconductors, both of which have been sold off. Galvin wanted to ensure that customers had various alternatives for its products under the Motorola tent. Rather than see them go to its major competitor, Zenith Electronics, also located in Chicago, Motorola created many overlapping and sometimes competing divisions. If one Motorola division could not make a customer happy with its product, another could modify the product or create one to customer specifications. This adaptability spurred further Motorola growth and created great customer loyalty. Motorola was also one of the first companies to put the customer at the center of product design and creation.

Nevertheless, this business model of competing and overlapping business units fostered significant political warfare within the company. This model was continued under Robert Galvin, son of the founder and the longest-serving CEO in the company's history. As the company mushroomed and corporate officers found it more difficult to manage and mediate between the different divisions, the need arose to organize related divisions or business units under a larger organizing function, which was called the "sector." Motorola was one of the first corporations to create the sector business unit. Each sector had its own president and a full set of support functions, including human resources, legal, marketing, and finance. Each sector was like a Fortune 500 company unto itself, except that it did not issue its own stock and was still accountable to corporate headquarters, which functioned more as a holding company. The sectors even sold products and parts to each other. At one point, Motorola had as many as seven different sectors and numerous divisions within each sector. This was the extent of "consolidation," as the emphasis continued to be on maintaining many different and overlapping business units. Any attempt to merge different divisions into a single business unit was met with strong resistance, not just within the sector, but at corporate level, too.

Motorola also had an aversion to outsiders and anything "not invented here." On one occasion, a sector president was recruited from the outside. He struggled for three years to earn his spurs with his own sector and with corporate. The reason that George Fisher was accepted as an outside recruit to the CEO's role was that he had started his career at Motorola. When Fisher resigned, the board looked outside the company for a replacement, and that created a firestorm. There was heavy lobbying inside the company, and several sector presidents demanded that Fisher's replacement should come from within the company. Gary Tooker, the executive vice president and former president of the semiconductor sector, demanded the loudest that he be promoted. Tooker was indeed made CEO, and under his brief reign Motorola began to lose market share. An outsider, Ed Breen, CEO of General Instrument, was made COO and president shortly after Motorola purchased General Instrument. He stayed just two years before going to Tyco. Breen could have succeeded Christopher Galvin, but he did not want to wait around, and his style did not mix well with Motorola's highly politicized culture.

Motorola's technology was held hostage by the company's political culture. At one point, the company needed to choose whether to migrate to a digital technology platform to support a new generation of wireless communications devices or remain with analog technology. The battles were public and loud. Eventually, a sector general manager who was heavily invested in analog won out, but the company lost. In the time taken up with the political battling, Ericsson and Nokia rapidly instituted digital and started taking away market share. In the course of a few years, Motorola went from being number one in wireless communications to number three.

When I joined Motorola's $3 billion, 26,000-employee wireless sector, I was charged with merging two competing business units into one global business—clearly going against tradition. I soon learned why an outsider was chosen for a task that no one in-house wanted. The wireless sector (also known as land mobile products sector) comprised the original Motorola business created by Paul Galvin. As a result, it had a lot of tradition and history that other sectors could not claim. This sector not only created products that continued to link police cars and dispatchers (as well as other types of fleet transportation with their dispatchers), it also created wireless systems that linked oil rigs with their regional and headquarters offices, and it also pioneered the first wireless connection between computers within offices.

The two divisions that I was charged with integrating, competitors on a global scale, were as different as night and day. As remanufacturing units, they each upgraded established Motorola products that were still in great demand. The newer division outsourced much of the actual production work while engaging in design and engineering. The older, established division had five times as many employees and maintained a traditional production line. The newer division made money; the older division lost money. (It had been a cash cow.) The older division also had had the same general manager for thirty years and was staffed with many well-established managers. They had created the division and what was once an excellent manufacturing process. They were at a disadvantage, however, in that they were under pressure from corporate headquarters to remake and update products for customers to the new Six Sigma standards. This was not always easy or appropriate for their products. As a result, they were no longer able to deliver products on time or within budget. This was not a problem for the newer division, for it was not constrained by Six Sigma requirements because it used outside manufacturers. When the two divisions were asked to merge, the older division resisted. Ultimately, corporate headquarters ordered the merger, which constituted a new direction and precedent. I rarely saw such resistance and outright hostility between two newly merged business units, and I have been involved in a number of integrations. The older division and its management were truly locked into a decades-old history and tradition which they found hard to relinquish. Many areas of the merger eventually fell into place as key support functions such as marketing and transportation came together. However, there remained two different production channels that could not be merged until leadership roles were settled. I decided to base succession purely on the results of the key managers from their former divisions. It became clear that most of the managers from the newer division would step up to run the merged division. There was politicking at all levels within and outside the sector and going up to the board. As the outsider, I was demonized, but as a consultant, I was accustomed to it. Within a year, the division was again a cash cow for the sector but the bloodshed was terrible. Most of the executives who lost their positions had to be given positions teaching and doing research at Motorola University until they reached retirement. Motorola's tenure system (another cause of political battles) made if almost impossible to lay off or fire management staff. Unceasing politics at Motorola cost the company its leadership position in the industry that it created.

I have found in my executive team consulting that excessive politics is a major contributor to the dysfunctional culture at the executive level, and it always ripples down into the organization. When companies exhibit a political culture, I know to start my investigations by looking at the top. In transforming a political culture into a service culture, I emphasize consensus building around commonly shared goals and values that raise the company's strategic needs above those of the fiefdoms and their feudal bosses. This is one area where I encourage dismissing executives who cannot bury their hatchets in order to attain the common good. Otherwise, the excessive politics can lead the company down a slippery slope to something like the Kmart situation, where the company takes on a frozen culture.

BUREAUCRATIC CULTURES

Say the word "bureaucracy" and immediately size, structure, lack of urgency, and mindless complexity come to mind (as well as a few expletives deleted). Nevertheless, I am convinced that *bureaucracy is a state of mind, not just size and structure.* Bureaucracies have become the bane of modern society for consumers, loyal company workers, managers, and those at the top. What bothers me most about the subject of bureau-

Figure 4.6

BUREAUCRATIC

PROCEDURAL
RIGID
REGIMENTED
AUTHORITARIAN
DEMANDS
CONFORMITY

****

GOVERNMENT AGENCIES
UTILITIES
INSURANCE COS.
BANKS
HMOS
CREDIT REPORTING COS.
PUBLISHING
TELECOM INDUSTRY

cracy is that we, in the business world, point our fingers at governments for their unresponsive and seemingly self-serving bureaucracies—at all levels—while ignoring the ever-burgeoning bureaucracies of the business sector. In the government sector, bureaucracies exist to enforce a wide range of laws, regulations, and policies ranging from the insignificant and the ridiculous to important matters of local and national governance and security. As citizens, we have enacted these laws, regulations, and policies through our public officials, and we expect them to be implemented and enforced—fairly. Thus, the bureaucracy. The business sector claims that it could do with less of its own bureaucracy if it were not burdened by government regulation. Anyone who has attempted to correct a bill for wireless service or tried to maneuver his way through an auto insurance claim knows otherwise. The same applies to obtaining customer support from an ISP or the company that sold him their latest high-tech gadget or computer. Workers struggle with the mind-numbing requirements imposed on them by their companies, whether it be to requisition supplies or to obtain information from the IT department.

Industries that are known for maintaining bureaucratic cultures include banking, power generation (utilities), telecom, insurance, and health maintenance organizations. At in-service seminars that I have conducted, respondents to questionnaires also included hospitals, airlines, and cable companies as bureaucratic offenders. Most of these industries are highly regulated or retain vestiges of their former regulated existence.

A number of factors have contributed to the rise of the corporate bureaucracy. In no special order, they include:

REGULATION. Yes, American business has to deal with regulations and laws—like the rest of us. Often, those regulations and laws are created in response to corporate misconduct. As a result, companies have to create bureaucratic structures that can respond to those regulations on behalf of the company. It should also be recognized that a number of industries have used their collective might to deregulate themselves (financial services, airlines, and power generation, for example) in pursuit of greater growth and profits, only to fail or to engage in fraud.

MERGERS. As we create larger business organizations through mergers, we create larger bureaucracies. While many employees are laid off in the wake of a merger, a larger, more complex organization has still been created. Bureaucracy has become a mechanism for managing ever larger organizations. In their groundbreaking book *Beyond Human Scale* (Basic Books, 1985) Eli Ginzberg of Columbia University and George Vojta, former vice chairman of Bankers Trust, warned that American business is creating outsized business organizations that might be too big to thrive. Larger organizations entail greater inefficiencies through increased scale, and the scale limits their ability to respond to a more turbulent business environment.

CONTROL. Management's fear of losing control is a major contributor to the growth and maintenance of bureaucracies. As result, decision making is highly controlled and centralized. Managers and executives create rules and policies (many more than are required) to maintain control and authority through the bureaucracy.

TECHNOLOGY. "I knew I would be screwed by a computer one day." So says fictional American president Josiah Bartlett in NBC's television drama *The West Wing*, in a reflection of a common paranoia. The computer and new communications systems have been touted as a means of reducing bureaucracies and creating greater efficiencies. But the increasing complexity and diminished reliability of technology (in response to our demands) have also made entire organizations hostage to it. That, in turn, has forced the creation of huge and costly IT departments. We all know what happens when the system goes down. The IT department has become another layer of bureaucracy in companies.

THE LEGAL DEPARTMENT. Legal departments were created with the original intention of proactively keeping the company out of trouble. In many cases, that means that normal operations are slowed or obstructed as the lawyers are consulted. Unfortunately, many companies ignore the advice of their legal departments or they fail to notify their legal teams of actions that might create downstream legal problems for the company. With the recent rise in corporate malfeasance, the corporate legal department is also being used as a screen for companies and their leaders to hide behind.

AVOIDING MISTAKES. Due in part to the corporate legal department, as well as an increasing aversion to risk taking and making mistakes, companies have created mechanisms to avoid and correct mistakes. These people who warn, monitor, check, and correct have become imbedded in our corporate cultures and add to the bureaucracy.

CORPORATE LEADERSHIP. Despite their cries for less bureaucracy, the typical corporate leadership cadre has wrapped itself in a cocoon of bureaucracy to put more distance between itself and the company's stakeholders.

Companies with bureaucratic cultures are usually mature organizations. Time and growth also contribute to rising bureaucracies. Companies with bureaucratic cultures do have well-developed, formal missions and business plans, but they are rarely implemented with any success. There is a huge reality gap between the mission and how the company actually performs. The leadership of bureaucratic cultures is usually slow and unresponsive to marketplace challenges and opportunities. Leadership is also risk averse and, many times, authoritarian. Most corporate leaders, as well as their subordinate managers, feel trapped by their own bureaucracies. When they do want to take action, they get tripped up by their own bureaucracy. Employee commitment is usually directed first to a function or department rather than to the larger company. There is reduced initiative and virtually no risk taking or innovation. People within bureaucracies have a diminished sense of urgency. If people within the bureaucracy are pushed to be more responsive, they take on the characteristics of a predatory culture and will retaliate, especially against those who criticize the bureaucracy. Team building is limited by structure, hierarchy, and rules. Not surprisingly, operating practices are highly rigid and procedural. Bureaucratic cultures have their own jargon, which is rarely understood outside the organization. Terms such as "analyze," "research," "review," "migrate," and "escalate" are just a few of the more common terms found in bureaucratic cultures. Strikingly absent are terms such as "taking action," "commitment," "urgency," "it was our fault," and "I will be responsible." Fitting into the larger bureaucratic scheme and complying with demands for conformity take priority over taking responsibility and working with a sense of urgency. No one single person can be responsible when issues and problems are circulated through many in and out boxes and across many different desks. As a result, accountability and performance are low in bureaucratic cultures.

Bureaucratic cultures are well known for their rigid hierarchies and convoluted structures that serve only to fragment and delay work flow and effective worker cooperation. People who move to a bureaucratic culture from a more service-oriented culture liken it to working with blinders on, or handcuffs, or "in cubicles with ten-foot-high walls and no exit." *Bureaucratic companies require more meetings of their employees. The meetings are necessary to overcome the bureaucratic structure, hierarchy, rules, and roadblocks that are endemic to the bureaucratic culture.* Meetings allow people to peek out over their ten-foot-high cubicle walls to find out what is going on in the rest of the organization.

Because companies with bureaucratic cultures are so inwardly focused, they are prevented from responding quickly and effectively to crises or changes in the external competitive environment. Those who interface with bureaucratic cultures complain about the lack of competence and absence of motivation by employees.

People working within bureaucratic cultures have few incentives to go beyond and above the call of duty and may even be punished if they do so. *By subordinating the needs of the customer to the needs of the bureaucracy, bureaucratic cultures turn once-loyal customers into consumer militants while driving away the best and brightest talent.* As a result, they are poor performers that rarely measure up to expectations.

[CASE STUDY]

When Murphy's Law Collides with a Bureaucratic Culture, Disaster Follows

On August 14, 2003, at 2:13 P.M., the entire northeastern United States was blacked out, along with parts of Canada. All residents and businesses in northeast Ohio; parts of Michigan, Pennsylvania, Maryland, and New Jersey; southern New England; northeast Canada; and all of New York were thrown into darkness for as much as three full days. An improbable chain of events created the "perfect blackout."

Nothing quite on this scale had ever happened before in the United States. At first, it was thought that the blackout originated in Canada. But that proved wrong. While a number of causes were later identified, it was soon determined that First Energy Corporation (FE) of Akron, Ohio, had quite literally fallen asleep at the switch. Thousands of pages of published investigative reports provide a step-by-step, minute-by-minute rundown of how the blackout occurred and what happened in the course of those three days in August 2003. Here is a brief, and nontechnical, review of the event:

1. Somewhere within the regional grid, someone or something dumped 300 megawatts of power onto the grid, overloading it. To this day, no one has been able to determine the source.

2. When an overload occurs, power companies "drop load" to avoid damage and wider blackout. FE needed to drop 1,500 megawatts, as the overload was in their area of control. FE failed to drop the load in the Akron-Cleveland area, a response that would have stopped the power outage that quickly rampaged throughout the northeast.

3. When this kind of emergency occurs, both visual and audible alarm systems are triggered in the operating control room so that operators know immediately what to do. However, FE had not properly maintained both of its alarm systems, so operators did not know what was occurring, and they could not drop the load in time. Neither monitoring system was fixed until after the blackout.

4. The alarm systems are monitored and triggered by a computer system. FE was in the process of updating its computer and software systems, but it delayed getting the new systems up and running in a timely manner. The slow migration to the new system created gaps in the computer system.

5. When FE failed to drop the load, a cascading effect ensued, causing its kilovolt-line system (sagging under the heat produced by the overload) to start to fail.

6. Then there was failed vegetation management. (I love this term. When I first heard it, thought it meant that a company's management had assumed a vegetative style. I have adopted this term for my own use in other parts of the book.) A major priority of electric utility companies in spring and summer is to manage or trim back tree growth—vegetation management. If this work is ignored, sagging power lines (heavy with electricity) short out when they come into contact with trees. FE had failed to maintain its vegetation management activities, and a tree branch touched a line.

7. The failure in the kV-line instantly created unsustainable burdens on connecting lines in adjacent areas and in a cascade they quickly spread as generator units auto-tripped throughout northeastern America. The blackout was on.

When we look behind these events at the cultural and management failures, we gain a different and more in-depth understanding of what triggered the blackout.

With the deregulation of the electric power industry, resources and priorities shifted to the unregulated-markets side of power companies. This was essentially the selling, buying, and trading of power, where profit margins are not regulated. For decades, power companies had been functioning within a regulated-market environment. This meant that they had built up large bureaucracies that were attuned to responding to regulatory requirements to ensure the safe generation and sale of power at fair market rates, as well as compliance with regulations. This is the normal and appropriate function of a bureaucracy—checking, monitoring, and complying. Now utility companies were rushing pell-mell into a brave new world of profit making. What they did not understand was that they still had bureaucratic cultures, and they still had responsibilities on the regulated side of their businesses.

Here is what was learned about management failures at FE:

1. The North American Electric Reliability Council (NERC) published reports on standards for managing voltage instability in various areas, including Akron-Cleveland. These were called reliability standards. They included actions to be taken to avoid and to respond to these conditions.

2. First Energy management ignored warnings by NERC and the Ohio Public Utilities Commission of these necessary standards and potentially dangerous conditions.

3. By failing to obtain the reliability standards, and by failing to implement education programs for appropriate personnel, FE planners were deficient in their understanding of the potential risks.

4. This, in turn, meant that FE operators were not aware of the consequences and were totally unprepared to deal with the chain of events that occurred.

5. FE was operating on the edge as it was unaware of NERC reliability standards and potential disruptive scenarios. This left FE with few options to deal with these disruptive scenarios, which became disastrous.

Since the blackout, compliance with reliability standards has become mandatory.

First Energy represented the worst of two cultures. Its regulated culture had fallen down on the job and took its job for granted. Financial resources were being diverted from the regulated business to support the growth of the nonregulated business. This was typified by FE's failure to put in place new computer systems that could have triggered alarms—assuming there had even been properly functioning alarms to sound the warning. It had trimmed its budget for field maintenance, which included vegetation management. Just as important, FE ignored necessary education and training required for its operators. First Energy's management had ignored the still critical regulated side of the business—power generation. It also ignored a complacent, bureau-cratic culture, which led to disastrous conditions throughout the north-east region of the country. In reality, First Energy's management had become vegetative.

Bureaucratic cultures exist for a purpose. However, even bureau-cratic cultures have to be improved and maintained and given the nec-essary resources required to effectively meet their goals. In its fascination with the new, unregulated side of the business, First En-ergy's management ignored the culture of its regulated business and it cost them and many consumers who were not even customers of the company. As Kim Wissman, deputy director of the Ohio Utilities De-partment, so aptly stated, "The competitive environment overloaded the system."

What all of these cultures have in common is their inward focus, which leads to poor performance if not failure. Most of us have worked for one of these cultures, and we have all had to deal with one or more of them as consumers. As employees, we have a responsibility to try to change the culture from within. As consumers, we have a responsibility to try to change the culture as external change agents. We will talk about culture change in chapter 8.

5

HIGH-PERFORMING BUSINESS CULTURES

Business has responsibilities beyond making a profit for their shareholders. We have important responsibilities to our employees, suppliers and to the welfare of our larger society.

—David Packard, Cofounder, Hewlett Packard

As we move up the Hierarchy of Cultures, we cross a barrier that separates high-performing cultures from all other cultures. I never miss an opportunity to ask managers and executives why it seems to be so difficult for companies to cross this invisible, yet seemingly impenetrable, barrier on the way to building a better culture. This question seems to be as difficult to answer as defining the term "culture" itself.

THE SERVICE CULTURE

The service culture is the first of what I call "cultures of change," or high-performing cultures. Companies with service cultures focus on exceeding, not just fulfilling, the needs of the customer in order to reach their own business objectives. Service cultures do this through fair and ethical sales practices and through excellent after-sales customer support. *In particular, they solve problems for the customer, and they do not make their own customer support part of the problem.* The true service culture has a mission, strategy, structure, systems, policies, and operations that are built around the customer. *Service cultures have a clear, outward focus toward the marketplace. They measure their own performance in terms of feedback from the marketplace—the customer.* The five cultures that we discussed previously have the opposite perspective in that they have an inward focus and usually ignore marketplace demands until there is trouble.

The service culture also has a leadership and management team, as well as a workforce, that puts the customer at the center of planning and operations. Companies with service cultures recognize that they are in the business of providing service, regardless of the product they make. Put another way, they recognize that the product will not sell itself without service and *service is what keeps the customer coming back.* In her efforts to turn around Xerox, CEO Anne Mulcahy has established a basic service principal for the company, "... the toughest competitors are the ones that embed themselves in customer relationships. It's never just about what they sell. It's about the trust that they've established with the customer." *Business Week,* August 21/28, 2006. True service companies are also attuned to changes in the marketplace. While service cultures do not always create change, they do recognize and respond to change quickly and effectively. *They are change-ready cultures. Rather than resist change, like so many companies, they embrace it to better serve customers and enlarge their market share.*

Westin Hotels, Manpower Inc., Jet Blue, and Whole Foods are examples of companies with outstanding service cultures. None of them invented their industries or the products they sell, but they went beyond their competitors to make their products more appealing through outstanding service. This type of value-added service has allowed them to take market share away from the competition and, in most cases, lead a niche within their industry. At the same time, they created a very loyal customer base. Despite the troubles in the legacy airline industry, Con-

Figure 5.1

SERVICE

CUSTOMER
FOCUS
QUALITY FOCUS
AUTHORITATIVE
RESPONSIVE
TO CHANGE

****

HARLEY-DAVIDSON
EDWARD JONES
JET BLUE
UNIVERSAL FIBERS
NEW BALANCE
TIMKEN CO.
WESTIN HOTELS
TARGET
CARDINAL HEALTH
EMERSON ELECTRIC
LATEX INTERNATIONAL
CONTINENTAL AIRLINES
MANPOWER

tinental Airlines is increasing its market share by focusing on improved customer service that has been identified by J.D. Power and Associates as the best among the legacy carriers.

The service culture is not limited to traditional service industries. A common misconception is that manufacturing companies cannot have strong service cultures. I disagree. Such manufacturers as Harley-Davidson, Johnsonville Foods, Timken Company, Johnson Controls, Emerson Electric, and pharmaceutical distributor Cardinal Health are also preeminent service companies, as they have built their success on exceeding customer demands.

[CASE STUDY]

A World-Class Manufacturing Company Sets the Pace as a Premier Service Company

Harley-Davidson was founded in 1903, and through the first half of the twentieth century was the global leader in motorcycle manufacturing. HD also grew to become an American icon. In the late 1970s and early 1980s, Harley-Davidson was flirting with failure as competitors from Japan were dumping motorcycles on the American market at artificially low prices. H-D asked the U.S. government for protective tariffs to allow it to regain its competitive edge in the American marketplace. H-D was very successful in regaining its competitive edge and in 1987 asked the government to remove the protective tariffs on foreign bikes—before the date they were scheduled to expire.

By the 1990s, Harley-Davidson could not keep up with customer demand for their world-famous "hogs." While most companies would be happy with that situation, H-D was not pleased with the delayed delivery time of cycles to its customers. Neither was the company satisfied with the experience customers were having with some of its dealerships around the country. H-D management found that some dealerships were taking unfair advantage of customers, causing management to implement new standards for quality service and fair conduct for all dealerships to follow.

H-D management was not satisfied to just change the conduct of its dealerships. It recognized the need to improve its own performance and culture. In 1993, the company initiated the "circle organization." Its purpose was to overcome a number of internal barriers in order to improve organizational and business performance, by

1. Eliminating waste by promoting collaboration and interdependence over internal competition

2. Overcoming difficult project start-ups

3. *Improving the company's ability to meet customer needs in a timely and predictable manner*

4. Improving how employees felt about their work, especially since the company was doing well

5. Supporting individual growth and excellence

6. Replacing their former hierarchical organization with a flatter organization organized around functional leaders

The three interlocking circles of the Circle Organization were designed to:

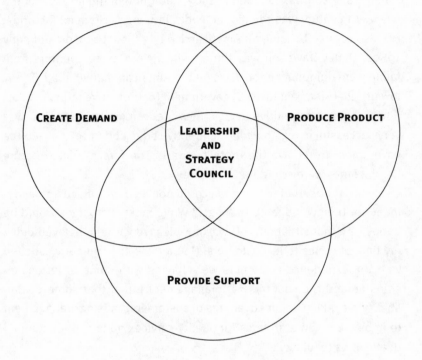

CREATE DEMAND

PRODUCE PRODUCT

LEADERSHIP AND STRATEGY COUNCIL

PROVIDE SUPPORT

Where the three circles met in the center was the Leadership and Strategy Council. Its principal function was to provide support to the company—not dictate to it.

The overall focus of the organization is directed externally on the stakeholders of the business.

As part of the Circle Organization, Harley-Davidson initiated what it calls the "Performance Consulting Group." This team of consultants visits dealerships to ensure that they are living up to Harley-Davidson's high standards and to help them meet those standards when they are having difficulty. The dealerships actually pay for the consulting service. The Performance Consulting Group's audits include the dealership's financials, customer satisfaction levels, and the conduct and performance of sales personnel. *Just as significant, Harley-Davidson continues to create an experience for the customer, not just a product for the marketplace; consumers are drawn to both the experience and the product.*

Harley-Davidson continues to drive its R&D division, which continually develops new engine technologies and new bikes. H-D even patented the trademark sound of its engine to prevent competitors from copying it. Through technology, H-D has been able to create a wider variety of bikes that appeal to a more varied riding public—including those who would not normally see themselves as motorcycle riders. This includes smaller bikes that have allowed H-D to penetrate foreign markets that do not have the expansive open roads of America.

Harley-Davidson also created the Rider's Edge—a riding course that helps would-be bikers become comfortable and skilled in riding a bike before actually buying the bike. The program even licenses them through the same training course. Women now make up 10 percent of Harley's customer base, and about 40 percent of the company's growth comes from women customers. The company is proud of its program that reaches out to prospective Hispanic and African-American bikers with sponsored events. In the process, Harley-Davidson has closed the production gap between orders and delivery time, where there was once as much as a nine-month wait for a bike. Harley-Davidson has grown far beyond its original Hells Angels customer base to serve a diversified customer base spanning wealthy executives, moms and pops, and a lot of riders in between. Harley-Davidson is an extremely profitable company and has earned it by putting the customer at the center of its business strategy.

Dave Baldwin, director of organization development for Harley-Davidson, and a former Ford employee, likes to say that "a terrible day at Harley-Davidson is better than the best day at Ford."

The Fortune 100 heavy-equipment manufacturer Caterpillar has learned that it can even out the boom-and-bust cycles by expanding its services to customers to include remanufacturing of engines as well as logistics and financial services (like GE credit). It has found a way to remanufacture old equipment, with high quality built in, to resell at lower prices to an expanding Chinese market, where the customer is usually not able to afford newer equipment. This manufacturing behemoth that once epitomized old-line manufacturing has demonstrated the value of providing service to its customers, and it does it by thinking about how it can satisfy customer needs.

Conversely, because a company is in a traditional service industry does not mean that it automatically has a service culture. We have all dealt with so-called service companies that do not understand that they are in the service industry. Banks are among the worst. Their beancounter mentality, combined with an excessive operations culture, prevents most of them from becoming strong service companies. Wachovia Bank spends millions on advertising that touts its outstanding customer service, but the ads contain fine-print disclaimers that tend to undermine the rhetoric. MCI was once known for having an innovative and highly responsive service culture. Bernie Ebbers killed that unique culture, and the company never regained it, even after the board replaced him. The new management simply did not try to return the company to its former roots as a strong, innovative service company. Comcast has taken for granted its protected status in most markets. It has one of the deepest and most complex management bureaucracies of any company I have ever experienced in the corporate world.

The best service companies know that innovation can make a major contribution to their service operations. Starwood Hotels, owners of Westin and Sheraton Hotels, is an excellent example. The company even has a chief creative officer, Scott Williams, whose job it is to promote innovation within the company. Starwood strongly believes that it has to innovate to keep from becoming just another hotel chain. As an example, it created the "Heavenly Bed" for the Westin Hotel chain, and it draws rave reviews from guests.

Toyota USA launched the Sienna minivan with children in mind. So who did they talk to? Kids, of course. Many of the things they learned from the kids went into the Sienna, including a soccer team–friendly total of fourteen cup holders and three temperature zones.

Jeneanne Rae, cofounder of Peer Insight, a service-innovation consulting firm, feels strongly that effective and innovative service is no accident and is built upon four platforms:

1. Leadership: Senior leadership should be driving the agenda about what is important for serving the customer

2. Culture: Organizations need to strive for a culture that accepts failure and promotes learning, and not just the validation of existing ideas.

3. Customer-centered innovation and development process: The organization must put the customers' needs at the core of design thinking and processes.

4. Infrastructure: Companies need to establish a governance structure for innovation that includes substantial budgets, internal know-how, and a set of trusted outside third parties for research, design, and prototyping.

To maintain their customer-centered outlooks, most service cultures value and empower their employees. Whole Foods empowers store team members to select products and hire new employees without input from management. Employees also determine who is promoted through elections—the ultimate 360-degree evaluation. That is also how H-D runs its business units. Corporate staff are minimally involved. Companies with strong service cultures recognize that their employees are the critical link between the business and its customers.

Companies with strong service cultures have a broader view of their stakeholders. This means that customers, suppliers, and employees are key stakeholders in the business, just as shareholders are. As a result, new hires more easily fit into service cultures because they are hired for their commitment to the customer. To ensure their success, new employees are also well trained and educated for their new assignments and are given every opportunity to fit into the culture.

Decision making and communications are more open and decentralized in service cultures to reduce delays in serving the customer. Employees are empowered to solve problems for customers without excessive guidelines, policies, and authority from above. People know how to access resources, and they have the authority to address customer needs. This means that the structures of superior service companies are usually flatter and less layered.

They are less rigid and hierarchical and have a minimum of bureaucracy. Where bureaucracy does exist, it is segregated from customer service operations.

[CASE STUDY]

Giant Food—The Decline of a Service Giant

For many years, the Washington, D.C., area has been known as a strong service town (excluding the government sector). Until recent years, it was not known as a corporate headquarters town for traditional businesses and industries, like other major cities. Its economy was built around the government, associations, and a number of home-grown service companies like *The Washington Post,* the Marriott Corporation, and Giant Food as well as a number of midmarket to small companies rarely known outside the area. In recent years, many of those companies were purchased and became subsidiaries of larger acquiring companies, or they lost their identity altogether. Giant Food was one those companies.

Giant Food was started in 1936 by N. M. Cohen and Sam Lehrman. Their goal was to create a chain of food stores around the D.C. metro area that would "meet all of the grocery shopping needs of area residents by providing a wide range of high-quality products supported by great service." For decades, Giant Food was where Washingtonians shopped. It became a Washington landmark. Indeed, Giant's high-quality products and exceptional service made it virtually impossible for larger, national chains to break into the affluent Washington market. When Cohen and Lehrman retired, Isadore "Izzy" Cohen (son of the founder) assumed the CEO role. He continued the same tradition and added more services. Under his leadership, Giant was one of the first grocery chains to create the supersize grocery store that included deli markets along with expanded product lines and services. It was known as Super Giant.

Giant was recognized around the nation as an outstanding grocery chain and an outstanding service company. Interestingly, Giant built its reputation for outstanding service in a competitive environment in which they had virtually no competition for decades. Izzy Cohen became a legend within the industry, and Giant was repeatedly recognized as the outstanding grocery chain in the nation by its industry retail association. Just as important, Giant had profit margins that were the envy of the industry. Customers most liked the service they received. Like a smaller mom-and-pop market, Giant store managers would order special items for customers when requested, and store employees went out of their way to make sure that the customers had a great shopping experience. If the customer could not find an item, she was taken to it by a store associate—and not just pointed to an aisle. Nor was it unusual for customers to talk directly with Cohen during his frequent store visits.

Giant was also a good place to work. It welcomed unionization. Employees were well paid, and there was no history of union-management conflict. Cohen valued input from employees and made sure that store managers worked cooperatively with employees. There was little turnover, and many employees spent their entire careers at Giant. Training was also important, as management invested heavily in programs to promote understanding and serving the customer.

Izzy Cohen died in 1995. For a while it looked as if the company would remain independent and remain true to its reputation for outstanding products and service. But in 1998, the family-dominated board sold Giant to the U.S. division of the Dutch grocery conglomerate Ahold. Ahold USA in turn transferred management of Giant to its Stop & Shop chain of Quincy, Massachusetts. Of course, Stop & Shop management made the usual commitments that it would maintain Giant's reputation for outstanding products and service, but Stop & Shop itself did not measure up to Giant's long-held reputation. Under Stop & Shop management, Giant's reputation began to erode.

Stores were no longer consistently stocked. Customer requests for items were ignored. At times, it was difficult to believe that any two different stores were both in the same Giant chain. Too frequently, items were incorrectly marked (a chicken might be marked with a flank steak label and muffins labeled rye bread). Store directories were persistently wrong and sent customers to the wrong aisle. Baskets were hard to find on entering the store. The computerized self-checkout lanes were excessively complicated (requiring the customer to look at three different screens) and plagued with problems. When the computerized self-checkout failed, a shopper couldn't get help.

I interviewed four different store managers and asked them why it was now so difficult to find items in the stores. They answered, each in their own way, that they no longer had control over inventory to respond to customer requests. They had lost control of their stores to centralized management in Quincy. Eventually, the distribution center in Lanham was closed, and truck drivers were laid off in favor of drivers from the Quincy distribution center. Homegrown Giant management staff in Lanham were also laid off.

Employees had become noticeably less helpful. Instead of taking customers to find items, they leaned on their elbows and pointed to aisles across the store. This is not entirely surprising, as Stop & Shop had a relationship with the union that moved in lockstep with Safeway. Management had no interest in having a better relationship with its workforce than its closest competitor or in paying its workforce just a little bit more to earn their loyalty. When a new labor agreement was negotiated in 2005, negotiations were acrimonious. Both Safeway and Stop & Shop forced labor to accept reduced benefits and wages for future employees in exchange for keeping their current wages and benefits. (Employees did have to shoulder more of the cost of their medical benefits.) The marketplace was not blind to the changes. In a survey of 573 Giant customers around the D.C. area, 398 said, "Yes, service at Giant Food is not as good at it was several years earlier." Only 46 said it had improved. Asked "Can you get the products you want the great majority of the time when you shop at Giant?" And 240 said no.

I decided to talk directly with Bill Holmes, executive vice president of operations, Maureen McGurl, senior vice president of human resources, and Marc Smith, CEO of Stop & Shop/Giant. When I asked McGurl and Holmes about the decline of the Giant brand, they had little to say. They did express their concern about Wegmans entry into the marketplace. Wegmans has just two stores in the Greater D.C. area (and none in Maryland) located in remote rural areas. They offer an entirely different kind of shopping experience—very high end, with many luxury items in an oversized store twice the size of the largest Giant store. Wegmans provides a "shopping experience" over practicality. It is not unusual to see people touring Wegmans as tourists—not shoppers. Holmes's and McGurl's biggest concern should have been the gradual but steady loss of market share to Safeway and North Carolina–based

Harris Teeter. When I spoke with Marc Smith, he sounded genuinely concerned but noted "the chain was in decline before we bought it." I quickly responded, "But, Marc, you have owned Giant for nearly six years. Isn't it time for you to take responsibility?" The most senior executives were going through executive handholding with a consultant but were doing nothing to try to change the culture of business down through the organization.

Since Giant Food was purchased by Ahold and its management transferred to Stop & Shop, the chain has lost 25 percent of its market share in the Washington, D.C., region, and customer complaints have increased dramatically. Investment bank analyst Robert Vos of Fortis Bank has predicted that the chain will "never return to its former level of profitability" (*Washington Post,* February 28, 2006). As a backdrop to these failures, the parent company, Ahold NV, was hit by an accounting scandal as well as the theft of confidential workforce personnel data through employee negligence and Marc Smith was dismissed.

Companies with strong service cultures recognize that employees and customers are integral to their success. Rather than being diminished by management, they are valued and relied upon for valuable feedback which allows the companies to keep pace with change.

THE NEW AGE BUSINESS CULTURE

Many high-performing cultures are also New Age cultures. This unique type of culture actually creates change in the marketplace, frequently by creating new markets, not just new products. *I use the term "New Age" because they exhibit an entirely new set of behaviors, values, qualities, and characteristics in the course of conducting business that would be alien to the cultures discussed in chapter 4.* Companies having a New Age culture combine innovation with a strong sense of urgency to change the marketplace—and to their advantage. They have an intense sense of commitment to the customer. They are also highly democratic, and, as a result, decision making is driven down into the organization. More accurately, New Age cultures have a bottom-up approach. New products and innovations come from within the company not from above. Employees have an opportunity to become wealthy as profits are generously distributed throughout the organization. Nearly a third of Google employees are millionaires or billionaires. It is no surprise that workers have a high degree of autonomy in making decisions. Risk taking is also very common, especially when the company relies heavily on innovation and creativity. Terms more commonly associated with this culture include: "can do," "blue skying," "innovation," "no barriers/no walls" (sometimes literally), "competence," "bottoms up," "breakthrough," "collaboration," "self-initiative," and "intreprenurial." Nevertheless, New Age cultures are not for everyone. In their formative stages, they are notoriously unstructured and unpredictable. Titles are unimportant; competence and one's contribution matter more. They frequently resemble chaotic cultures.

New Age cultures are also noisy and self-critical. You sometimes need a tough hide to work in a New Age culture. Organizational communication may be haphazard or at the least unlike the more formal and controlled communications found in traditional companies. Rites and rituals, rules, policies, and practices are informal, or are in the formative stages of development, while myth building is becoming important as people make important breakthroughs.

In fact, these characteristics do describe many high-tech companies, including Cisco Systems, Google, SAS Institute, and the former People-Soft, to name just a few. Nevertheless, the New Age culture is not associated exclusively with high-tech companies, and many of them do not have New Age cultures. In no way do companies like Oracle, Unisys, Nortel, and the Microsoft of today exhibit characteristics of New Age cultures. Many companies outside the high-technology sector do have New Age cultures, such as Southwest Air, Nucor Corporation, Patagonia, Emerson Electric, Green Mountain Coffee Roasters, and Johnson Controls. These companies invented new ways to go to market as they created change in their respective industries. They also developed very different relationships between management and their workforces where employees were seen as true stakeholders in the business.

The New Age culture exhibits some of the characteristics and features of the service culture through its commitment to the customer and empowerment of its workforce. *The New Age culture is unique, however, for its ability to translate innovation into business performance as well as for its ability to create change in the marketplace.* Under their legendary founder, Herb Kelleher, Southwest Air turned the commercial airline industry on its head by eliminating the hub-and-spoke system. Their reservations and check-in systems are totally different (and more democratic) from the legacy carriers. Nevertheless, it has been the carrier's business culture that has endeared it to the marketplace. Southwest has forged an intense bond with its customers by creating a new flying experience. Management also fostered an open and egalitarian relationship with its employees. Southwest leadership also demonstrated a unique sense of foresight in its practice of purchasing jet fuel for years going forward at current prices. Most of the companies in the industry are flying bankrupt while Southwest is still making money. Patagonia encourages its employees to spend time outdoors—not indoors—testing its outdoor gear and to come up with new ideas for new products.

Figure 5.2

NEW AGE

CREATES CHANGE
INNOVATIVE
EGALITARIAN
CONSENSUAL
QUALITY FOCUS
LONG-TERM
FOCUS
ENTREPRENEURIAL

****

SOUTHWEST AIR
NUCOR
MICROSOFT (1980S)
SAS INSTITUTE
GOOGLE
GREEN MOUNTAIN
COFFEE ROASTERS
JOHNSON CONTROLS
PATAGONIA

Nucor Corporation—A New Age Business Thriving
Amid Industry Failure

Nucor's success can best be summed up as an escalator ride up while the rest of the American steel industry rode an escalator down. American steel has been in decline since the early 1970s for a number of reasons, including: Detroit's replacement of steel in auto manufacturing with increasing amounts of lighter metals and plastic; periodic labor unrest; and dumping by foreign companies onto the American market. Like the airline industry, the steel industry has also hurt itself by its reluctance to transform the way it conducts business—including how it makes steel. Also like the airline industry, most of the steel industry's companies have been bankrupted. U.S. Steel, for decades the largest steelmaker in the world, is no longer the largest steelmaker even in the United States. That distinction belongs to Nucor.

A Different Business Model

Nucor was the butt of industry jokes and skepticism in the 1960s and 1970s for the way it made steel, but no more. Traditional steel mills, called "hot mills" or integrated mills, rely on enormous quantities of iron ore, coke, and coal to make steel. The integrated mills (famous for their blast furnaces) are also more labor intensive. Nucor invented the minimill process, which eliminates iron ore and coal. Instead, Nucor melts steel scrap—nearly twenty million tons of it annually—through an electrification process. This process has many advantages:

1. It is less costly.
2. It does not require expensive iron ore or coal to be mined and shipped to the mills.
3. It is environmentally cleaner, since cold mill production does not put as many pollutants into the atmosphere.
4. It is not as labor intensive as a traditional hot mill.

Nucor is also the largest recycler in the nation, and much of the 20 million tons of scrap comes from more than five million recycled autos. Increasingly, more steel companies have become converts and have switched to cold mill manufacturing.

Nucor prides itself on being the low-cost, high-quality producer of steel for industry.

A Unique Management-Workforce Relationship

The company's unique management philosophy was started by Ken Iverson, who took over as CEO in 1966 when the company was not as prosperous as it is now. He instilled the notion then that if the company was to be successful, management had to be there to support and serve its workers as well as its customers. Nucor management allows employees to earn based on their productivity and ingenuity. That, in turn, should allow employees to know that they will have a job as long as they contribute. Employees know that they will be treated fairly. If they feel they are being treated unfairly, they have a systematic appeal process that forbids retaliation. One of the more prominent characteristics of New Age cultures is their bottoms-up approach to decision making and getting the job done. Nucor is a prime example of this philosophy.

Nucor has the highest-paid steelworkers on earth while maintaining the lowest labor cost per ton produced. Base pay is low, but incentives are high, ranging from 80 percent to 150 percent of base compensation for production workers. As a production company, Nucor puts its production workers ahead of management and white-collar workers. Office workers are also eligible for bonuses, which are set at 30 percent of base pay as measured by the performance of their divisions. Production workers know that high absenteeism will hurt their own earnings potential as well as their team's, so absences occur only for the most legitimate reasons. Nucor's absenteeism rate is under 1.5 percent. Employees also have an ownership stake in the company. The focus is on quality production and controlled costs.

Egalitarian Compensation and Benefits

Nucor also has an "egalitarian benefits system." What this really means is that management has the same benefits as employees. Management does not have better vacations or insurance plans, and they do not have company cars, corporate jets, executive dining rooms, and reserved parking. Many employee benefits are *not* open to officers, including profit sharing, scholarship programs, service awards, and employee stock purchase plans. This all adds up to very low turnover, and that also reduces costs.

Technology Leadership

To support workers, Nucor invests heavily in new technology and equipment. The company seeks new technologies that will enhance quality and production while improving safety. The company is even conducting research into eucalyptus trees as a possible alternative fuel source that would be cheaper and cleaner. Of course, Nucor made the minimill production process a reality for the entire industry. Nucor also has one of the very best safety records in the industry, and it backs it up with excellent training. Nucor has also demonstrated that New Age cultures need not be chaotic. Nucor's work environment is orderly; it lacks the chaos and frenzy seen in many high-tech companies that have a New Age culture. Much of that orderliness can be attributed to the need to maintain a safe work environment.

Well-informed and Enlightened Managers and Leaders

Management recognizes that its success is based on its 11,000 employees, and it seeks to hire and retain only the most talented and productive people. Management has battled "bureaucracy creep" and maintained a simple organizational structure. Just recently, it added a fifth management layer, based on recent acquisitions. The flat management structure encompasses

Supervisor

Department manager

Plant manager (general managers and vice presidents who manage the production plants)

Officer (only thirty-one for this Fortune 500 company)

CEO

When you visit corporate headquarters in Charlotte, North Carolina, you find an office environment that does not bespeak the usual Fortune 500 style and cachet as there are very few headquarters staff and even fewer administrative staff. Executives assume a lot of their own secretarial support responsibilities. The lean work environment that has become a popular catchphrase in the business world is practiced at Nucor's executive offices, but nothing is spared to support workers in the production plants.

Interestingly, senior officers do not have employment contracts. They can be dismissed at will. Even their famed, longtime leader of more than thirty-five years, Ken Iverson, was not above being dismissed in 2001. Nor do executives participate in any pension or retirement plans, and their base salaries are lower than those of executives in comparable companies. The only other compensation they receive is a bonus (paid in cash and stock) based on Nucor's annual overall percentage of net income to stockholders' equity.

Exceptional Customer Service and Quality

Nucor has distinguished itself as the leading producer of the highest quality steel through its uncompromising commitment to quality, competitive pricing, and highly responsive service to its customers. Customers are treated as partners. Many Nucor plants are ISO 9000 certified. Most important, Nucor does not see itself as just a steel producer. It knows that its real business is its commitment to every customer with every order. It is a service business first and foremost.

Corporate Culture and Performance

All of these factors add up to a high-performing culture and a high-performing business. Still, there are other contributors to Nucor's New Age culture that are not built into the company's policies. For example, employees, over time, can fire a supervisor. If a supervisor is wrapped up in his title and authority, he or she is not likely to last long. If a supervisor is considered to be a hindrance to worker effectiveness and productivity, he is removed. The most successful supervisors know to listen to workers, recognize good ideas they put forward, and provide whatever support they can for their workers. The best managers are helpers, not bosses. Nor are the rank and file afraid to speak up with criticisms or ideas that may improve productivity. According to Jim

Coblin, vice president of human resources, "Managers know that their employees will make them successful. They are servants to the hourly worker."

Typical of a New Age culture, Nucor's management and workers are keenly aware that they continue to have challenges. Among them are China, with its government-supported steelmakers, the formation of larger overseas conglomerates with lower labor costs, and the need to hire better-educated workers as required by increasingly sophisticated technology.

While manufacturing in the United States continues to decline, Nucor continues to ride the up escalator, as both its stock price and earnings for 2005 reached record levels. That is the trademark of a true New Age business culture.

WHEN NEW AGE CULTURES TURN TO THE DARK SIDE

Maintaining a New Age business culture does not happen by itself. Many companies that once had a New Age culture lost it. Microsoft may be the most conspicuous example. Through the early 1990s, Microsoft exhibited many of the characteristics seen at Nucor or Google. Microsoft had a truly democratic work environment that was highly innovative and had few rules; structure and hierarchy were unimportant. It also created an entirely new marketplace with its Windows software for computing. But as Microsoft became a Fortune 50 company in the mid-1990s, it became obsessed with controlling, not just its own market, but others that were only tangentially related to its own. Some say this grew out of Bill Gates's obsessive need to control the planet—any market that was driven by software. That need to control competitive conditions grew into monopolistic practices, and a number of other companies decided to push back through federal lawsuits. Microsoft was also slapped down in Europe for the same practices, and in late

2005 Korea hit Microsoft with large fines for illegally bundling its products.

More revealing has been a growing chorus of criticisms from within the company, accompanied by major defections of some of its top talent. These include an intimidating culture led by CEO Steven Ballmer, declining innovation and risk taking, stock options that have lost their value, and a mushrooming bureaucracy. These are all signs of a maturing company in which scale has killed off its former culture. Just as important has been the reduction in vacation time and benefits, coupled with smaller bonuses at a time when the company continues to earn huge profits.

Some say that Google is starting to exhibit similar behaviors as it expands its empire. Like Microsoft, it is also being criticized for its willing collusion with the Chinese government to restrict free speech over the Internet through technology. More telling may be its slowing creation and implementation of new technology (*Business Week,* July 3, 2006), which may be attributed to the chaotic nature of its culture.

Conditions that can kill a New Age culture include:

- Success
- Leadership that is no longer a good match for the New Age culture
- Size: bureaucracy
- Too much chaos
- Age of the company

Nucor has demonstrated that it has overcome all of these potential trip wires, especially the issue of age. It has maintained its New Age culture for nearly forty years. It will be interesting to see if Google will have a New Age culture in thirty or forty years.

6

ADDICTIVE BEHAVIORS WITHIN THE CULTURE

In individuals, insanity is rare, but in groups, parties, nations and epochs, it is the rule.

—Friedrich Nietzsche

Behaviors within a business organization are pervasive and constitute a major contributor to its culture. The behaviors of individuals drive organizational behavior and ultimately determine a company's performance. Organizational behaviors are reflected in the manner in which workers interact with each other, their customers, superiors, subordinates, and suppliers. In the age of technology-aided work, it may be feasible to include our interactions with technology. A company's goals and objectives as well as its policies also influence how people behave within the organization. Hard-charging companies that impose extreme demands on their workforces to continually produce will foster hard-changing people. Companies that make few demands of their employees will have a workforce that lacks urgency, innovation, and an ambition to succeed. Bureaucratic cultures promote bureaucratic behaviors on the part of their employees. *Nevertheless, no one wants to talk about behaviors, especially those who sit on mahogany row. Apparently, a discussion of behavior is a taboo subject in work environments akin to politics, religion, and sex.* The exception is when the company decides to dismiss an employee and any discussion of behavior is purely one-sided and self-serving for the company. At that stage, it is too late to be dealing with behaviors. For that reason, I am openly addressing the subject in this book.

Understanding the behaviors of an organization and its employees is critical for comprehending the culture and for undertaking any culture change initiatives. Part of the problem is that business managers do not recognize that behaviors can be measured, but behavioral scientists do so routinely. In reality, people within a business organization do give informal feedback to each other on what is acceptable and what is not acceptable. One of the first things that new employees do, on entering a new workplace, is to sample the climate for behaviors that are acceptable and unacceptable so that they may act within those norms.

I should note that I am not the first person to use the term addictive behaviors in relation to the business organization. Anne Schaef and Diane Fassel extensively talked about addictive behaviors in their groundbreaking book *The Addictive Organization* (Harper & Row, 1988). I have encountered ten major categories of addictive behaviors at work within organizations: *conformity, denial, projection of blame, obsessive-compulsive behavior, passive-aggressive behavior, punishment, politicking, excessive careerism, ethical convenience,* and *hubris.* I use the term "addictive" because people continually rely on them and make them a part of their behavioral repertoire within work environments to the exclusion of more positive and productive behaviors. Of course, organizations themselves display many of these behaviors. Where appropriate, I will also attach these behaviors to the different types of cultures that were discussed in chapter 5.

1. CONFORMITY

When we first attend school, as children, we want to fit in. Conforming is a means to achieve acceptance (in extreme environments, conformity may actually help us survive). The same applies in many work environments. In fact, when we first report to work in a new company, we are encouraged to start doing things the Pepsi way, the Intel way, or the HP way. Conformity is good in that it helps to create cohesiveness and esprit de corps within the organization.

Unfortunately, many organizations' demands for conformity become excessive. People are expected to leave their sense of initiative, honesty, and integrity at the front door. This was the case at Enron, where people well down in the organization were widely engaged in corrupt behaviors, just as their senior executives were. Enron bred a culture of lawlessness.

Companies with bureaucratic and frozen cultures are cathedrals to conformity. In large part, that is what makes their cultures bureaucratic and frozen. Widespread organizational conformity causes a bureaucratic culture to react to change slowly and a frozen culture not at all. When people try to speak up with a better idea or to criticize an accepted norm, they are usually snubbed. If they continue to buck conformity, they can be forced out of the organization. This also deprives the organization of what may be valuable feedback and potentially innovative new ideas. Excessive conformity forces the most talented workers to take their careers elsewhere. The worst outcome of conformity is that it gives people within the organization a false sense of security when the company may be moving toward disaster.

2. DENIAL

As soon as we are able to talk as children, we begin to engage in denial when we do something wrong. Denial is a natural defense mechanism to protect ourselves from blame and harm as well as from mistakes. As children, we have not yet developed a sense of integrity and responsibility, and we find the world around us to be unpredictable and threatening. Much of our behavior is shaped in childhood, and most of us have had a healthy and normal upbringing that allows us to take responsibility for our behaviors.

Something seems to happen when we go to work. Many of us temporarily put aside the positive lessons that we learned during childhood. We will acknowledge our mistakes at home and accept criticism from our spouses and friends, but not at work. Part of that may be attributed to demands to conform as discussed in the previous section. More of it comes from the company's fortress mentality. We see our CEOs deny responsibility for wrongdoings of the company, so we engage in the same behavior as a defense mechanism. Corporate attorneys tell employees, and the CEO, to deny responsibility—when they know the situation is otherwise. At the end of his career as CEO of Merck, Raymond Gilmartin persistently denied that Merck had engaged in any misrepresentation or wrongdoing regarding its arthritis pain drug Vioxx. The same sorts of denials were issued by his counterparts at AIG, Marsh McLennan, Arthur Andersen, Adelphia, Cendant, and many more. As his criminal trial approached, former Enron chairman Kenneth Lay undertook a carefully planned public relations tour during which he spoke out in defense of himself. Lay even set up a Web site. His principal defense was that he could not be held responsible for the behaviors of his subordinates and employees if he was not aware of what they were doing. If the chairman of the company cannot be held responsible, who can be? That is denial in the extreme.

3. PROJECTION OF BLAME

"Projection of blame has become an epidemic in organizations as well as larger society. As finger-pointing becomes more widespread in the general population, it should be no surprise that more and more employees are taking this behavior with them to the workplace" (J. Want, *Managing Radical Change: Beyond Survival in the New Business Age,* Wiley, 1995). Quite simply, projection occurs when an individual is found to be wanting in his behavior, performance, or unfulfilled responsibilities and, rather than take responsibility for his own conduct or mistakes, projects blame onto the accuser. The most common form of projection of blame is in accusing the complaining person of being rude. When pressed to describe the behaviors that were so rude, they cannot. This is becoming an increasing problem as we expect fewer phone workers to serve more customers. Management has the false expectation that technology can compensate for dwindling numbers of workers. Quite the opposite occurs. Office workers are also sources of projection of blame. Caught between an outside party and their boss, whom they cannot easily blame for his failure to provide direction, administrative and secretarial employees find it easier to blame the outside party, even if it is a customer. Many times, this type of projection of blame arises out of an employee's sense of powerlessness.

This has become an increasing problem in the retail customer-service realm, where phone centers have become the hub of so many businesses. Internet service providers and other phone-centered businesses are prime examples. In most cases, the customer service representative has little training, little supervision, minimum accountability, and even less incentive to work with the customer to meet her needs. They also have something else—anonymity. When a company rep does not have to face the customer or show an ID badge, he finds it easier to dismiss the customer—or worse. Phone abuse by both customers and company employees has risen dramatically. Dell Computer has paid a heavy price for its poor after-sales customer support: Some customers are going online to complain and warn others. Customers do not like being abused by Dell customer support representatives just because they express dissatisfaction or anger at the unprofessional and widely incompetent "service" provided them. What puzzles me about Dell's response is that they have offered to provide upgraded customer support—for those who are willing to pay extra for it. That also goes to the company's arrogance. Companies themselves just do not value customer-service operations or the people who serve in this largely thankless function. In the business world, Verizon may be one of the worst for combining poor customer support while projecting blame on to the customer. Neither Ivan Seidenberg nor any of his subordinate officers seem to care about their persistently poor customer service. Some customers who have expressed dissatisfaction say they have become the object of retaliation by employees, who have failed to correct errors in bills or even disconnected service.

4. PASSIVE-AGGRESSIVE BEHAVIOR

Passive-aggressive behavior is closely associated with projection of blame and is widely encountered in the work environment. It is the sneak attack when least expected. It is the politely worded refusal to comply with policy, requests, or complaints. People who feel that they are not empowered in the workplace frequently rely upon passive-aggressive behavior to make a point. Companies with alienated and failing cultures (see the bottom right quadrant of Business Change Cycle in Figure 1.3) are filled with employees who look for opportunities to sabotage the boss or the company.

5. *OBSESSIVE-COMPULSIVE BEHAVIOR*

Obsessive compulsive behavior reflects an inability or unwillingness to abandon the status quo. Frozen and bureaucratic cultures find it hard to release themselves from failed practices, values, missions, and policies. It should be no surprise that the employees also have trouble as they obsessively commit to outdated practices and compulsively engage in the same behaviors. Managers and executives also engage in obsessive-compulsive behaviors. Their most common obsession is with power and authority. An obsession with work reflected by long hours at the office or plant is worn like a badge of honor. Many production companies are so obsessed with operations that they overlook larger organizational issues, especially the culture.

6. *PUNISHMENT AS A TOOL*

The business world has never been shy about punishing workers. In recent years, however, as a result of federal and state workplace rules and laws, companies have become more circumspect in how they mete out punishment. Nevertheless, companies and their managements still find ways to bring employees back into the fold or to keep them from working anywhere else again. Predatory and highly political cultures are well known for their overreliance on punishment as a means of control. This creates widespread mistrust which, in turn, reduces innovation and team building. Many times, punishment is a direct outgrowth of a leader's outdated belief systems about how to manage and lead people. Larry Ellison of Oracle, Stephen Ballmer of Microsoft, Maurice

"Hank" Greenberg of AIG, Bernie Ebbers of WorldCom, and Frank Lorenzo, former CEO of Continental Airlines, have all been publicly accused of using punishment and intimidation against employees. Nor is it a coincidence that turnover in those companies was so high under each CEO. Considered by many in the insurance industry to be its most towering figure, Greenberg's management style pushed company executives to engage in bid rigging, among other fraudulent practices that led to the company's indictment and Greenberg's firing.

7. POLITICS AS USUAL

With the exception of American political institutions, no social system is more political than the corporation. Office politics exist in virtually every business organization. Political cultures, however, take politicking to a different level as the conduct of a company's business is characterized by game playing, deal making, coalition building, and constant political maneuvering. Workers in political cultures put politics above best professional practice. Decisions are made based on politics and coalitions rather than on market needs and demands. *When a company puts politics before business, it is doomed to failure.* Shortly after taking over Motorola, Ed Zander became so fed up with the politics, he started firing people; he told those who remained that if they could not stop their political infighting, they, too, would be thrown out of the company. Much of a company's political environment is created by the people at the top. For some, it is a conscious component of their management style. Again, Larry Ellison of Oracle comes to mind. Others simply cannot manage the politics. Joe Antonini of Kmart is a prime example. Politics cost him his job and led to the company's downward spiral.

8. RAMPANT CAREERISM

Excessive careerism is a particular form of politics that is played out in almost every type of work environment. It is especially apparent in firms that have an "up or out" culture, as in the major management consulting firms, investment banks, and some of the major high technology firms like Microsoft and Oracle. We have all known people who will step on anyone who is in their way in order to get to the top. Many of them do rise, and, of course, a manager does not rise to the highest level of a company without putting his career first. When Jeffrey Immelt was chosen to succeed Jack Welch at General Electric, a number of other Fortune 500 companies, among them 3M and Home Depot, had their pick of GE presidents who had lost the CEO sweepstakes. They left when they did not reach their goal of becoming Welch's successor.

9. ETHICAL CONVENIENCE

When the employees of a company feel that they have license to engage in unethical and illegal conduct, the business is doomed. We have all listened to the tapes of employees at Enron laughing about their own fraudulent activities. We now know that audit partners at Arthur Andersen not only helped Enron conceal its off-the-books debts, they engaged in similar practices for other companies, including Sunbeam, among others. Other more subtle forms of ethical convenience can include character assassination, revising history, or just doctoring a résumé or the books. The increasing pressure to produce, to be promoted, or plain greed has forced many ethical individuals to stray at all levels of organizations. Dennis Kozlowski and Bernie Ebbers shamelessly enriched themselves at the cost of their companies and did not believe that they could be held responsible. Most bothersome about such cases is that their boards of directors allowed it to happen. What about *their* sense of ethics?

10. HUBRIS

The Oxford American English Dictionary defines hubris as "1. arrogant pride or presumption. 2. excessive pride toward or in defiance of the gods leading to nemesis" (Oxford University Press, 1999). The problem with many corporations and their leaders today is that they think they are gods and are beyond criticism and accountability. At present, American society is dependent upon our regulatory and legal institutions to rein in corporate hubris. Only a few corporations—those with service and New Age cultures—have opened themselves up to outside criticism as well as internal criticism. American business has to build more New Age business cultures or American business may be at risk. We already have seen the failure of entire industries that held themselves above reproach to the very end.

STEPS TO CHANGE THE ADDICTIVE CULTURE

I will be dealing in depth with strategies for culture change in subsequent chapters. Here special attention needs to be given to the issue of changing addictive cultures.

The addictive behaviors of workers and managers are best handled on an individual basis. Sometimes a skilled manager or human resources representative can assist the employee or direct him or her to outside resources that deal with addictive behaviors that negatively impact their performance or the performance of others around them. Mentoring and coaching is becoming an increasingly necessary responsibility of managers, so they have to be prepared to deal with the addictive behaviors of their subordinates as well as their own. Frequently, the leadership team needs to come to grips with their own addictive behaviors before the larger organization does. I have found that many executives respond well to the mentoring and coaching process and replace addictive behaviors with more positive and productive behaviors that benefit the entire organization.

Dealing with the addictive behaviors of an entire organization requires a different type of intervention—a serious reality check. The organization may be functioning under a false sense of reality, where the culture has substituted its own sense of reality for what the outside world sees. Companies that have been indicted for lawless behavior in the marketplace have been functioning with a set of addictive behaviors. The other types of cultures that we explored in chapter 5 all have their own repertoire of addictive behaviors. Therefore, *education is the first step in helping the addictive culture rid itself of its addictions.* The culture needs candid feedback from the outside. This may come from customers, suppliers, or shareholders. On some rare occasions, a board of directors will bring in new leadership to confront the company with its need to discard its addictive behaviors. *The second step is to replace old constructs* (deeply held belief systems) with more functional constructs or behaviors. Feedback from the marketplace with alternative behaviors is also beneficial. It may also include benchmarking companies that have positive, performance-driven cultures that are relatively free of addictive behaviors. *The third step requires consensus building.* At this stage, a growing consensus must be built for desired alternative organizational behaviors. True consensus building takes time and is not a matter of just compromising. I will talk more about consensus building in the next chapter. There may be people, departments, or groups within the organization that resist the change effort. They are still wedded to their addictive behaviors. They need additional, intense assistance or leaders within the resistant group may need to be separated from the company. *The final step requires action.* The organization needs to test alternative behaviors that it has agreed upon. Schaef and Fassel, authors of the book *The Addictive Organization* (Harper & Row, 1988), even advocate that companies undertake the twelve-step approach followed by Alcoholics Anonymous for ridding alcoholics of their addictive behaviors.

For decades the consulting firm Booz Allen Hamilton was well known for maintaining a highly punitive and punishing culture. One component was a policy that compelled consulting staff on assignment to remain in the client company's office even if they were not consulting that day. (This allowed Booz Allen to continue billing the client company.) As the firm experienced significant defections of talent, discontent, and complaints from clients, they recognized the need to confront their addictions, and they started to change their culture. At the core of the culture change process were their behaviors. Managers and officers who were especially known for their heavy-handed ways were coached and counseled to change. Those who did not were demoted or separated from the firm. Better working conditions were also created for consulting staff, including more off-site office space so that consultants could conduct confidential research and directly access needed administrative support from the home office. Eventually, turnover declined, clients and consulting staff were happier, and Booz Allen once again began to attract and retain top talent.

If a company is to change its culture, it must directly confront its own addictive behaviors. Memos, restructuring, policy statements, and town hall meetings will not change a culture if they fail to address the painful issue of behaviors.

7

LEADERS AND CORPORATE CULTURE

Most of what we call management consists of making it difficult
for people to get their work done.

—Peter Drucker

I was meeting with the chief executive officer of a major service company to talk about the challenges that he and the company were experiencing. The CEO had been recruited from another service company the previous year, where he was the COO. His former company had a reputation as an outstanding service company that generated steady financial growth, and he gloried in its corporate culture. In his new company, conditions were different. There seemed to be problems everywhere, most of which could not be attributed to operational issues. At one point in the conversation, I asked him to describe the culture of his new company. After a few moments of thought, he responded: *"It's the eight-hundred-pound gorilla sitting outside my door."* It was a tellingly honest response. I only wish that other corporate leaders were so candid. When questioned about their company's culture, other officers have responded, "It takes care of itself" and "You should talk to human resources, it's not in my domain." At eBay, one senior officer commented to me: "We really don't think about the culture, here at eBay," indicating that culture is simply not an important issue to the company. When dealing with the subject of corporate culture, I have found that corporate leaders fall into one of three categories:

- I don't know.
- I don't know how.
- I don't care.

"In a sea of managers, the business world cries out for leaders" (John Gardner, *On Leadership*, Free Press, 1990). The business world has become fixated on managing and has elevated too many *managers* to the corner office where only true *leaders* should reside. Leaders today are tasked with managing risk, shareholder investments, new product development, mergers, downsizing, various crises, public opinion, and, of course, the bottom line. Few really understand how to lead an entire business organization, and that requires an understanding of the complex issue of culture. *In the age of radical change, increasingly complex business organizations require true leaders, not just managers.*

THE WRONG LEADERSHIP AND THE CONSEQUENCES

There are a number of reasons why leaders have difficulty dealing with corporate culture, including: the relentless pressure (by boards) to deliver on successive, short-term financial goals; the increasing size and complexity of today's business organizations; the desire and need to manage recurring crises; *and a lack of understanding of how to lead an entire organization—not just a business.* In recent years, leaders of business enterprises of all sizes have been more closely identified with self-enrichment and the misuse of power than with the enrichment and advancement of the business organization that they have been charged to lead. Part of the problem belongs to the larger society, as we retain too many outdated notions about the nature of leadership. Regardless of whether we are talking about business, government, or the nonprofit sector, we have given leaders unchecked power and status and have ceased holding them accountable for their actions.

We are also failing to develop the leadership needed for today's business environment. In preparing for this book, I examined the curricula of thirty first- and second-tier graduate and executive business school programs, around the nation, and found that *none* of the programs had a formal course that prepared future leaders to understand, develop, and lead a business culture. It is small wonder that corporate culture is assigned so little importance by today's business leaders.

LEADERS WHO DESTROY THEIR COMPANIES

My first, direct experience with predatory business leadership was with Frank Lorenzo at Continental Airlines. I interfaced directly with Lorenzo only once, and that was by accident. (He invited himself to the presentation of the final results of an organizational audit and angrily threw a pen in the direction of one of my partners who was presenting to the board.) Nevertheless, I saw the full effects of his "leadership" while consulting to the company at the behest of the board. Before Lorenzo took over Continental, the airline had a reputation as the premier American commercial air carrier. Its service and reliability were second to none. Lorenzo had had no previous experience in running an airline—or any other company for that matter—as his experience was principally as a Wall Street analyst. After he took over the company, it all went downhill. Initially, I was skeptical of the reports I heard about Lorenzo—his leadership style and what he had done to the company. For example, his own offices were protected by Plexiglas, and security personnel prevented anyone from visiting with him without going through security (it could be said that Lorenzo pioneered today's airport security system). The story turned out to be true. According to pilots, he reportedly said on a local Houston news broadcast that ground crew and flight attendants should not expect wages that would allow them to aspire to owning cars and homes and they should ride public transportation to work. Only when I saw the taped interview did I believe the story. Eventually, Lorenzo was thrown out by the board, as it was determined that he was harming the company, but the damage had been done. Lorenzo's actions and behaviors clearly showed that he had no interest in the culture of the company and that he was not part of it. In some ways, Lorenzo was the forerunner to similar unscrupulous practices by corporate leaders of today.

We have seen too many CEOs who have treated their own publicly traded companies as if they were the sole private owners. In so doing, they have fragmented and destroyed their companies through their own misguided leadership and turned companies into nothing more than their own personal bank accounts. Former CEOs such as Al Dunlap of Scott Paper and Sunbeam, Joseph Nacchio of Qwest Communications, Bernie Ebbers of WorldCom, Dennis Kozlowski of Tyco, and John Rigas and his sons of Adelphia Cable, became the real-life Gordon Gekkos of the business world. In some cases, their personal conduct actually led to the financial ruin of their companies. In just six months, between December 2001 and June 2002, Tyco's stock value lost 75 percent of its value. Bernie Ebbers ruined MCI, once a true New Age business culture that combined innovative business practices with outstanding customer service that changed the telecom industry. Alfred Taubman, chairman of Sotheby's auction house, and his counterpart at Christie's, Sir Anthony Tennant, conspired to fix auction commissions: In the 1990s they defrauded art sellers out of $400 million in commissions. Apparently, it was not enough that those two auction houses already controlled 90 percent of the market. Taubman was eventually convicted of fraud along with his CEO, Diana D. Brooks. John Rigas, founder of Adelphia, was also his company's ruination. Under CEO Joseph Nacchio, Qwest Communications lost 70 percent of its stock value between 2001 and 2002 and the company was fined $43 million by various state public utility commissions for poor customer service. At the same time, Nacchio was allegedly taking tens of millions of dollars out of the company for himself (he is now under indictment). The late Ken Lay, convicted on numerous charges of fraud, never seemed to understand that his actions killed the unique business entity that he created. This type of "robber baron" behavior contributes to a company's fragmentation by creating a superior class of employees (yes, corporate leaders are, in most cases, employees) with elevated privileges coupled with reduced accountability.

No Risk Taking at the Top

Rewards should be commensurate with the risk taken and the results produced. But too many of today's corporate leaders have insulated themselves from risk. Even their boards seem to promote this behavior, and—no surprise—almost all corporate boards today are composed of sitting and former CEOs, many of whom are handpicked by the company's CEO. We are just beginning to see corporate CEOs held accountable for their conduct. It is even more important that corporate boards should be held accountable. None of the Enron directors was convicted of anything, and they were responsible for protecting the company's investors.

Nor do CEOs and other senior executives share the risk as do the masses of employees. Even when fired, CEOs are richly rewarded, while downsized employees are often given minimum severance. CEOs are even rewarded with bonuses when they order a merger, regardless of the outcome, while employees lose their jobs. James Kilts, CEO of Gillette, was paid $105 million for engineering his company's acquisition by Procter & Gamble, and no one was more critical of the payout than board vice chairman Joseph Mullaney. In 2000, Kilts was paid $70 million for arranging the sale of Nabisco to Philip Morris. John Eyler, CEO of failing toy maker Toys "R" Us, will benefit to the tune of $63 million. Georgia-Pacific's A. D. Correll received $92 million for arranging that company's sale to Koch Industries, and Bruce Hammonds, CEO of MBNA, will receive $102 million when the credit-card bank is purchased by Bank of America, although Bank of America has policies against such bonuses. Like Kilts, Michael Capellas is a double winner, having been paid for selling both Compaq to Hewlett-Packard and MCI to Verizon. While CEO of Compaq, Capellas showed a distinct inability to reform a fractious and underperforming culture. With such sweet deals, companies are spawning a class of business "leaders" whose only motivations for leadership will be to broker mergers. This perpetuates the growing trend of making companies nothing more than monopoly pieces. Demonstrating competence as a leader of an entire business organization is no longer required.

Jill Barad, former CEO of Mattel, and Carly Fiorina, former CEO of Hewlett-Packard, are examples of CEOs who took their companies in the wrong direction but who paid no personal price for their failed leadership. Under Barad's failed direction, Mattel's stock lost more than half of its value, along with a comparable loss in market share. When fired, Barad was given a $59 million golden parachute along with lifetime medical coverage and car service. Fiorina received $42 million in severance and stock after her dismissal from Hewlett-Packard. All Fiorina had to show for her efforts were new advertising campaigns in the media and a failed acquisition of Compaq (along with a failed attempt to purchase Coopers & Lybrand's consulting business) while HP's market share and stock value declined. Neither of those two CEOs paid any attention to the cultures at the two declining companies.

Fannie Mae's CEO, Franklin Raines, was paid $99 million between 1999 and 2004, when he was fired because of the company's faulty bookkeeping and manipulation of earnings. The company had to pay $400 million to settle charges with the Securities and Exchange Commission. Based on an inquiry by former senator Warren Rudman, "Raines was faulted for fostering a culture that was obsessed with hitting earnings targets and took a fast-and-loose attitude toward accounting rules" (*Washington Post*, July 17, 2006). Between the end of 2004 and 2006, forty-four of Fannie Mae's top fifty-five executives left the company.

When American Airlines was in jeopardy of going into bankruptcy, former CEO Don Carty, along with his senior executive staff, attempted to protect their pensions and bonuses while at the same time negotiating billion-dollar wage cuts with the labor unions. When Ed Zander became Motorola's CEO, he negotiated as part of his contract that for each of the first five years he served as CEO, he would receive a fully vested pension plan, giving him five fully funded pensions at the end of just five years of employment. No other Motorolan, not even the company's five previous CEOs (three from the founding Galvin family), ever dreamed of such a deal. Famed management guru Peter Drucker advocated that no CEO should be paid more than 20 times the lowest-paid worker in the company, yet today the average CEO pay is 400 times that of the lowest-paid worker—and climbing. *Many CEOs today have transferred the risk to the average employee while insulating themselves from their own failures.*

BENIGN NEGLECT

Between those CEOs who effectively lead and invest in their company's business cultures and those CEOs who betray their company's cultures, there is a large gray zone for most other corporate leaders. They preside over their companies through benign neglect. These leaders avoid dealing with the business as an organization, and they dare not look too deeply into their corporate culture. Ivan Seidenberg of Verizon, Brian Roberts of Comcast, Tony Nicely of Geico, Dick Notebaert of Qwest, Jay Johnson of Dominion Resources, and Edward Whitaker, chairman and CEO of AT&T (formerly SBC), typify most CEOs who know that their corporate cultures are overly bureaucratic, slow to innovate, poor problem solvers, and unresponsive to the marketplace. They are the CEOs who say "I don't care" by the way they run their companies, and they are the CEOs who are always wondering why they cannot generate larger profit margins or reduce customer turnover. In many cases, they are *permitted* to ignore their cultures as they have monopolistic control over their marketplaces. They do not have to deal with competitors in truly open marketplaces.

THE RIGHT LEADERSHIP

"CHIEF PASSIONATE OFFICER"

Hard as it may be to find effective corporate leaders who understand and are committed to their company's culture, they are out there. On entering the Shelton, Connecticut, office of Michael Lorelli, the chief executive officer of Latex International, one notices a nameplate by his door: CHIEF PASSIONATE OFFICER. That pretty much sums up Lorelli's leadership style, which has gone far in reviving the fortunes of this wholesale manufacturer of latex foam products for high-end mattresses and pillows. Though he has led two Pepsico business units, including Pizza Hut, Lorelli does not demand the usual trappings seen in the of-

fices of most CEOs. His office is just a few steps away from the manufacturing plant. Neither does he have an army of executive assistants.
Since Lorelli took over Latex in 2002, the company's sales have increased more than 70 percent while the company has captured 18 percent of the specialty sleep sector. The company expects to grow its share
of that market by 75 percent by 2008, with eventual market share topping 55 percent. Nor does Lorelli spend a lot of his time on plotting
mergers. Instead, he is always finding ways to grow the company organically. That includes developing custom-made new manufacturing
technology that no one else in the industry possesses and expanding
plant capacity in the United States, which is functioning at 100 percent
capacity. Lorelli calls it "intelligently built capacity." When asked about
the company's culture, Lorelli makes clear that the culture starts with
the customer and the customer's needs. As a result, Latex International
is the only producer of Rejuvinite foam products, recognized as the
premier latex material in the industry. People at all levels of the company are called upon to put forward their best ideas, and at times, it may
even turn into a "food fight," but everyone is on the same team. Behind
the scenes at Latex, there is always a sense of team synergy impelling
Latex's performance-driven culture. The watchword of the culture at
Latex is "Get it done for the customer, let the employees have fun, and
make money"—in that order. While many claim that the U.S. manufacturing economy is in an irreversible decline, Latex is a thriving manufacturing company that maintains a thriving culture. Passion for the
product and the culture go hand in hand at Latex.

In the fast-moving high-tech world, companies seem to pass through
stages of the Business Change Cycle more rapidly than in other industries. As a result, it is not surprising to see companies with New Age business cultures quickly take on the characteristics of lesser cultures. I will
talk in greater detail about Microsoft's changing culture in later chapters,
but the company can no longer claim to have the characteristics of a New
Age culture, which it may have boasted in the 1970s and 1980s. Bill
Gates and Steve Ballmer's leadership styles have been totally incongruous
with the culture of an innovative, New Age, or service culture, and its top
talent is fleeing to Google and other high-tech companies. In addition,
company shareholders have not been making money on the stock.

*   *   *

One of the biggest challenges for companies with New Age cultures is to sustain them. Cicso Systems is one company that has maintained its New Age culture through tremendous success as well as the high-tech bubble of the early twenty-first century. In the 1990s, Cisco was the Google of its day, and it remains the leading Internet and telecommunications gear maker in the world. It may be said that without Cisco, there would be no Internet. Much of that achievement is due to its CEO, John Chambers. Chambers leads by example, not by demands and dictates, which seems to be the case at Microsoft, Oracle, Nortel, and SAP, among other high-tech companies. Cisco set out to build a culture that epitomized the New Age culture: strong collaboration and team building, high expectations and goals, high integrity among its workforce, pushing the envelope around new technology development, and a truly democratic workforce. In the age of Sarbanes-Oxley, Cisco is squeaky clean; it has not been dogged by antitrust suits as has Microsoft. When I interviewed Barrie Novak, director of human resources strategy and planning at Cisco, I was initially concerned about our means of communication, as I planned to pose questions via phone and the Internet, but she assured me that employees at Cisco had the freedom to speak their minds and that their phone calls and e-mails were not monitored or screened. This is a company whose leadership and workforce have implicit trust in each other. Like so many other hyper-growth high-tech companies, Cisco also created a number of millionaires during its earlier period of meteoric growth; it believed that the workforce should share in the company's profits. At the same time, employees have accepted the fact that when profits are thin, as they have been for the entire industry in recent years, there will be less wealth to share. Chambers himself has not collected a paycheck since 2001, and he has not pushed the panic button. Unlike Microsoft's increasingly restless workforce, Cisco's workers remain highly committed to the company and its future, and they do not experience many defections to younger, faster-growing Silicon Valley companies. The culture remains the centerpiece at Cisco, and much of that is attributed to John Chambers and the example set by his leadership team.

Other CEOs have demonstrated that paying attention to the culture makes good business sense. Jeff Joeress, CEO of Manpower Inc., turned that failing company into the world's second-largest staffing firm by establishing high service standards that became an integral component of the company's culture.

At Green Mountain Coffee Roasters, founder and CEO Robert Stiller watches with great satisfaction as his workforce drives the company's profitability, which averages 20 percent annual growth. At the same time, company employees took the lead in making sure that Green Mountain Coffee Roasters developed a sense of social responsibility that is virtually unmatched in the business world. They actually live their corporate mission:

[CASE STUDY]

Green Mountain Coffee Roasters Purpose and Principles (3/29/04)

OUR PURPOSE

Our purpose is to create the ultimate coffee experience in every life we touch from tree to cup—transforming the way the world understands business.

OUR PRINCIPLES

DECISION MAKING—At the most effective level. We speak timely, informed, criteria-based decisions aligned with our business goals. Our decisions are made with personal commitment, ownership and accountability.

LEADERSHIP—At every level. We develop leaders that demonstrate a high level of competence, generate trust and bring out the best in themselves and those around them.

COMMUNICATION—Open Dialogue. In our thriving, healthy organization, we share information, ideas and successes.

APPRECIATING DIFFERENCES—Finding opportunity in conflict. Opportunity comes from welcoming different opinions and ideas with mutual respect.

PERSONAL EXCELLENCE—Strong organizations rely on strong individuals. We are responsible to do our personal best for ourselves, our co-workers and our company. Personal excellence is built on a high level of skills, knowledge, self-awareness, self-motivation, and respectful intentions toward all.

BUSINESS SUCCESS—Financial Strength. We deliver steady growth in market share, sales and profit. Financial strength benefits employees, stockholders and communities worldwide.

CONTINUOUS LEARNING—For today and tomorrow. Our competitive strength comes from the continuous improvement of all that we do. We actively seek out and apply best practices.

VIBRANT WORKPLACE—A place where you can make a difference in the world. We create and maintain a culture that fosters teamwork, fun, personal growth, career paths, financial rewards and a healthy work-life balance.

ETHICS—Do the right thing. Integrity is the foundation of all our decisions, actions and relationships.

PARTNERSHIPS—Success for all. We collaborate with our partners for mutual benefit. Our relationships are based on respect, honesty, openness, reliability and trust.

PASSION FOR COFFEE—From tree to cup. We roast great coffees and are committed to ensuring that everyone who encounters Green Mountain coffee has an outstanding coffee experience.

PLANNING & MEASURING—To understand and improve. We focus on integrated planning throughout the organization to align our strategies. We gain insights into our successes and challenges by measuring and evaluating the results of our actions.

SHARED OWNERSHIP—Thinking and acting like owners. We meet our commitments and appreciate the contributions of each other. We are stewards of our collective resources. We share equitably in our success.

SUSTAINABILITY—Pathway to our future. We use resources wisely and make decisions that take into account the well-being of people, profit and the planet.

WORLD BENEFIT—Creating positive change. We are a force for good in the world. We celebrate and support the power of business and individuals to bring about positive changes, locally and globally.

Jeff Bleustein and his predecessor at Harley-Davidson, Richard Teerlink, turned that company around, in part, by building a new relationship between management and the labor unions. Their unique leadership has continued with their current CEO, Jim Ziemer. To this day, unions play a key role in the management of the company's various business units. In their small cycle division in Kansas City, there are no executive offices, but you will find a bull pen for the three leaders of the business unit—two union chiefs and the Harley-Davidson general manager and vice president, Ken Eberle. When the plant was first planned and built, Eberle and the union staff led the planning and site construction without corporate involvement. Jeff Bleustein and several of his headquarters staff went out to Missouri for the ribbon-cutting ceremony and then went back to their offices in Milwaukee.

Nucor, the nation's largest steelmaker, has had a series of New Age leaders, starting with Ken Iverson, who recognize that a production company needs to put its production workers first: It is a production worker's company. The workers have the opportunity to enrich themselves through their productivity and quality. *They even enjoy profit-sharing opportunities and a pension plan that are denied to management.* The board and leadership of that company recognize that the real risk takers are the production workers.

Neither Nucor nor Harley-Davidson advocated the draconian salary cuts that Robert S. Miller Jr. tried to implement at Delphi Automotive Systems, even though both companies went through their own difficult times. Miller tried to put the blame for Delphi's problems on the shoulders of its workers, but at Nucor and Harley-Davidson leadership recognizes that dividing their companies into opposing management and labor camps will only lead to their destruction.

In 2004, Motorola spun off its semiconductor business to become Freescale Semiconductor. Few gave it a chance to survive, much less thrive, given Motorola's culture of internecine warfare as well as fierce competition in the imbedded chip industry led by Texas Instruments. The division had also gone through a painful downsizing of nearly a third of its workforce between 2000 and 2001. New CEO Michel Mayer, who came from IBM, was not deterred, and has set a different tone for the company. He started by issuing stock to company employees and then set high standards for accountability and performance. Automatic raises have become a thing of the past. Raises are now based on performance—and average performance no longer earns an automatic pay raise or a bonus as in the past. Mayer also did away with the silos that previously prevented the free exchange of ideas, talent, and resources. Mayer insisted that people begin to work with each other and to share resources around the company. Mayer did institute one quality that Motorola had once been famous for but had long since neglected—putting the customer at the center of business. Customers are once again involved in the product design and development process, a practice that had made Motorola the industry leader in past years. By putting the culture front and center, Mayer has seen Freescale boost efficiencies and profit margins while the former Motorola culture characterized by political battles has been left in the past.

Whole Foods Market founder and CEO John Mackey has steered his company to the top of the grocery retail marketplace with extraordinary profits. Nevertheless, Mackey pays himself a salary of just $450,000, which seems appropriate for a company that prides itself for having a strong democratic work environment.

THE ROLE OF LEADERS IN CHANGING THE CULTURE

In the course of my consulting over the years, I have found that effective stewards and leaders of corporate culture demonstrate a set of qualities and beliefs that clearly benefit the company's culture as well as the overall performance of the business. They not only include CEOs but also other senior managers as well as middle and frontline managers who manage and develop the culture from within the organization. Nevertheless, CEOs have advantages that no one in the company can exercise. They include having the unique position in the company to command everyone's attention as well as their commitment to changing the culture. CEOs can also set the agenda and make available the resources required by the process. They can also help create coalitions, remove obstacles, and, most important, inspire people. In a word, *CEOs have the power to make culture change a reality*, if only they would use it.

1. BECOME A STUDENT OF THE CULTURE

A company's culture is not owned by anyone and certainly not by the CEO. It is the product of many contributing forces over the years, principally through people's behaviors, commitments, and values; the company's business practices, policies, mission, and history; and industry conditions. If a company's culture has not been consciously shaped and developed at the company's founding, it will probably have taken on a life of its own and will be even more difficult to change. Everyone within the culture needs to become a student of the culture before trying to change it. That includes the CEO.

Phillip Purcell, former CEO of Morgan Stanley Dean Witter, ignored that firm's culture at his own peril. Purcell led Dean Witter at the time of its acquisition by Morgan Stanley. The culture differences between the companies were striking, but Purcell ignored those differences. Morgan Stanley has always been a white-shoe investment bank. Dean Witter was a stock brokerage firm which had been owned by Sears, earning it the nickname "stocks and socks" for that unusual relationship. As a brokerage firm, Dean Witter catered to the needs of individual middle-income investors and the newly wealthy. A succession plan had been put in place after the merger by Richard Fisher, chairman and CEO of Morgan Stanley, who engineered the merger. It called for John Mack, COO of Morgan Stanley, to continue to run Morgan Stanley as the CEO and Purcell to serve as chairman. Purcell would follow Mack. Purcell did not want to wait, and he pushed Mack out and became chairman and CEO. Purcell ignored several protocols of investment bank culture, one of which was that the CEO, if called upon, would help "close a deal." A deal could be underwriting a merger or issuing an initial public stock offering. Each of these deals brings tens of millions of dollars to the firm. This same CEO involvement is not required in brokerage firms, as the nature of the business—selling and trading stocks—is quite different and properly left to brokers. Purcell persistently refused to involve himself in major deals, even when requested, and kept a clear distance between himself and the day-to-day operations of the business. He even spent much of his time in Chicago—the former headquarters of Dean Witter—rather than at the New York City headquarters of Morgan Stanley. Under Purcell's aloof leadership, Morgan Stanley's culture became increasingly bureaucratic, risk averse, and slow to react. Under Purcell, major decisions could take up to a year, forcing many key executives to leave in frustration. It was not long before Goldman Sachs replaced Morgan Stanley as the premier investment banking firm in the world. Eventually, the pressure from the Morgan Stanley side of the business forced Purcell's ouster and John Mack was brought back to run the firm. Mack has wasted no time in building a culture that is fast on its feet, as major decisions are made in days (and board members know that they have to be ready to give their approval quickly). In addition, people are encouraged to take risks (essential in investment banking). Purcell did not want to become a student of the culture and he failed.

On the other hand, one of the best students of corporate culture I have known was Howard Levin of Digicon Electronics. A hard-charging operations engineer, Levin was inserted into the troubled company by a board dominated by two merger-and-acquisition firms, so he had to deliver results quickly. Nevertheless, he took the time to understand the company as an organization. He even undertook the task of benchmarking the company's culture against companies with reportedly effective business cultures and not just in that industry. Only then did he start to make decisions about restructuring, promotions, and outside hires. At times, his board questioned his approach, but eventually he proved that his approach was the correct one. Every operational improvement and marketing initiative he undertook was linked to the new culture that he was building for the company. He was determined that the company would have a culture that would support enlightened leadership and, if necessary, survive poor future leadership. Over time, the student of the culture became the teacher as Digicon became an industry leader.

2. RENEWAL

CEO are uniquely positioned to make culture building a process of renewal. By renewing the company's culture, people's talents and commitments are reenergized on behalf of the company. I know of no downsizing, operations improvement, business process reengineering, or restructuring engagement that has had a renewing effect on a company; to the contrary, these measures have almost always put increased stress on a company's culture. At the height of CSC Index's consulting (the firm that started BPR under Champy and Hammer), it quietly started a search to buy a consulting firm that could "renew and heal our client companies' cultures" after they concluded their business process reengineering. Index's partners recognized that BPR inflicted such harmful effects on their client company's culture (not to mention day-to-day operations) that it required an additional follow-up intervention to renew the culture. That recognition spoke loudly of BPR's failure.

3. COMMUNICATIONS

CEOs and their change leaders must ensure open communications within the entire organization. Nothing can create more distrust than to shroud the culture change process in secrecy. When people feel left out, resentment and resistance will grow. Open communications within the change team is also essential so that people are on the same page and are also able to exchange new ideas and resources. Again, the CEO has the "bully pulpit." A major concern is when the CEO simply does not keep the organization informed. This sends a message to the organization that the CEO does not put a high priority on the change process, and that alone can undermine it. Communications from the CEO can also be used to inspire the larger organization (and the change leaders) and rally everyone to the cause.

4. INCLUSIVENESS

The CEO must make clear to the organization that culture building is an inclusive process. It should not set out to exclude people (except those who demonstrate their unwillingness to support the process) but must reach out to the entire workforce for their ideas and commitments. A major benefit is that it grows over time to embrace everyone. New leaders have to be welcomed into the process to expose new ideas and recommendations, and divergent ideas, too. A renewed culture cannot be imposed on the organization like a new software program or voice messaging system.

5. TRUST

CEOs have to instill a sense of trust among participants in the culture building process. People must feel it is safe to voice their opinions and differences about the newly envisioned culture and the way the process is to be managed. Trust between members of the change team is essential if the change process is not to be derailed. When issues of trust arise, the CEO, not a consultant, will be the best person to address those issues. Alan Phillips, CEO of family-owned Phillips Corporation, a precision machine parts manufacturing company based in Columbia, Maryland, builds trust by opening the books of the company to his employees. He also puts a great deal of value on supporting the company's culture. While competing in a shrinking American industry that is moving overseas, the company continues to grow. Phillips himself attributes its ability to remain competitive to the trust built up within the company between management and its workforce.

6. ACCOUNTABILITY

No single person is in a better position to hold people responsible than the CEO. This is where the CEO's sponsorship trumps that of any other officer in the company. Only the CEO (acting on behalf of the

board) can determine whether the culture change process is going in
the right direction and is accomplishing its true goals.

Leading a company's culture is every bit as important to a company's
success as leading the other components of a business. When a company's culture lacks leaders, the company as a whole lacks leadership.

PART III   CORPORATE CULTURE BUILDING IN THE AGE OF RADICAL CHANGE

8

A BLUEPRINT FOR CORPORATE CULTURE BUILDING

What we need is a new paradigm—a new vision of reality; a fundamental change in our thoughts, perceptions and values.

—Fritjof Capra (from his book *The Turning Point,* Bantam, 1984)

Just as corporate leaders have difficulty understanding corporate culture, they are equally perplexed by the culture change process itself. Corporate executives expect the process to be like other interventions when it is not. Other types of business interventions can be "done to the organization," through a newly issued policy or through the efforts of a relatively small group of experts (internal or external). Changing the culture of a business requires widespread employee involvement and buy-in. It also requires the right process. The change process does not deal with machinery, office supplies, or reorganizing an organizational chart: *Its focus is on people.* For example, various marketing, IT, or operations improvement efforts do not demand the widespread involvement of the workforce. Certainly, the people who work in companies do not have much of a say about new technology; it is handed to them by the IT department and they have to live with it. If Merck's frenzied marketing of Vioxx had been put to a vote by the entire work-force, it probably would never have left the laboratory. Too many managers reject anything that requires a *process*, though too many were quick to embrace (mistakenly) business process reengineering. The company has to do it for itself, even when a small group of experts are employed to advise and support the process. Memos, policy statements, town hall meetings, executive retreats, and management directives will not accomplish the task by themselves. They do not always involve leadership team involvement—just consent.

Developing a new strategic business plan is usually accomplished by outside consultants (or an internal strategic planning department) without the involvement of the larger company or even middle management. In fact, a major criticism of strategic planning is that it does not take into account the larger organization's ability to support the strategy.

How Not to Change Corporate Culture

One example of how *not* to change a company's culture was seen at Time Warner when Jerry Levin was still CEO and chairman. It was a year before the AOL merger and Levin decided that he wanted to instill in the company a renewed sense of mission while setting the direction for the "new culture" he believed the company needed. The company had lost much of its drive and sense of urgency, and growth was slowing. According to one officer, "The company had become one slow-moving bureaucracy." Levin's method with typical for a media company. He first convened several off-site meetings with his most senior executives to determine the new mission and culture the company should have. Then, Levin made a forty-five-minute video, starring himself, outlining his thoughts, and had it distributed to everyone in the company. The process stopped there. Since there was no involvement of employees, there was no buy-in. People's attitudes, commitments, behaviors, values, and competencies were not changed. Performance did not change. The workforce did not own the culture change process; instead, they were just passive video viewers. The alternative culture that Levin envisioned existed only in his mind.

Another, and possibly misguided, approach to culture building was initiated at General Electric in 2003. Its goal was to shed its long-entrenched engineering culture that had been so famously wedded to Six Sigma technology and replace it with a culture that was focused on innovation, greater autonomy, and the future. The task of changing the culture was not led by Jeffrey Immelt, the CEO, but instead was handed to the company's chief marketing officer, who in turn brought in a group of anthropologists to assess the culture and make recommendations. They were followed by consultants from several design consulting firms that help companies design new products. It was no surprise that many employees thought that the meetings were "a waste of time." As GE's new CEO, Immelt missed a great opportunity to put his own stamp on the culture change process.

WHERE TO START: CREATE SPONSORSHIP AT THE TOP

Some degree of controversy exists as to where to start the culture change process. Within the organizational consulting profession, many feel that it should start at the top of the organization. Others, like Gary Hamel, believe that it should be a bottom-up approach (G. Hamel, *Leading the Revolution*, Harvard Business School Press, 2003). I have concerns about any bottom-up approach that does not have the full commitment and support of senior management. I do agree that people within the organization need to own the change process and the culture, but strong leadership and sponsorship from above are required to avoid chaos and to sustain the process, especially when it inevitably runs into roadblocks. Unfortunately, we have not yet reached the point where corporate America allows a true democracy to work its will inside the company. The bottom-up approach assumes that success is not possible without first gaining a broad-based buy-in by the rank and file. I agree that full involvement and commitment by all levels of the workforce is crucial if the process is to be successful. Nevertheless, I know of few organizations where the workforce will take the initiative, of itself, for such a weighty project without approval and support from above. The bottom-up approach can be successful in very flat organizations and in employee-owned businesses. A potential hazard for the bottom-up approach is that if leadership changes or becomes threatened by the emerging new culture, the entire process can be derailed. New senior management may not be committed to culture building.

Verizon once made a halfhearted attempt to change the "culture of its middle and senior middle management ranks." The effort pointedly excluded the top twenty officers, whose behaviors were in complete opposition to the culture change efforts taking place in the management ranks just below them. Needless to say, the effort failed.

A top-down strategy recognizes that the process needs sponsorship at the most senior level if it is to be successful. It also signals to the organization that it is one of the most strategic needs of the company. *Sponsorship should clearly start at the top of the organization.* The culture change process will not succeed if the CEO and other senior officers do not wholeheartedly endorse the change process (and even the board of directors should proactively put their authority behind the change process). The CEO and his officer team need to communicate to the entire organization a strong sense of urgency about changing the culture. They also have to be a part of the change process themselves. If they divorce themselves from the process or put themselves above it, then they have already conveyed a message to the organization that it is not important. We have also seen that too many profligate CEOs and senior management teams have created a culture of privilege for themselves, what I call a "mahogany row culture." In too many such cases, it has spelled doom for the company as well as destruction of CEO careers. The CEO needs to make clear that he and his senior management team are a part of the culture, just like everyone else in the company.

A systematic and bias-free culture audit will give the necessary direction as to where to start the change process. Factors to be considered include the nature of the business, its organizational structure, marketplace demands, and, most especially, the unique conditions of the company's existing culture. At times it may be appropriate to start the process within a key division or business unit and then spread the process through the business. In extremely rigid and hierarchical organizations (e.g., telecom companies) it may be appropriate to start the change process at a particular organizational level. In highly regulated companies that operate in several states (again, telecom companies or power generation companies) it may be best to start within one of those state organizations. Bureaucratic, frozen, and chaotic cultures require a top-down process to signal that a resistant culture must change. Top-down strategies are also necessary in privately owned businesses and especially in family-owned enterprises. In these types of businesses, which have a paternal cast, the workforce always seeks permission from above.

GOALS FOR CULTURE BUILDING

The first step in any culture-building process should be to ask why undertake the process in the first place. This means identifying key goals for culture building initially by senior management but eventually it must include the broader workforce. Failure to do so will be a major impediment to the endeavor. If the leaders of a company cannot grasp what those goals should be and articulate them to the larger organization, then the process cannot move forward. If the employees cannot clearly understand what the goals for culture building must be, and how it relates to them and their work, they cannot be expected to commit to it. *This failure to understand the goals for culture building is a major reason why it is so rarely undertaken in the business world.*

The goals for culture building may differ among business organizations. *Nevertheless, the one universal goal for culture building is improved performance.* Too many corporate leaders and boards do not recognize that their corporate cultures are a major impediment to their company's success. Creation of a performance-driven business culture must be the paramount goal of the culture building process. Other important goals include:

INSTITUTING HIGH STANDARDS FOR ETHICAL CONDUCT is a must goal for culture building. Reinforcing these high standards of ethical conduct is important, even in companies that do not have apparent problems in this area. In a 2005 Roper poll, Americans were asked to rank organizations by their ethical conduct: Corporate leaders (and companies) came in last, behind the media and government. Nevertheless, ethics for the sake of ethics is not enough. Failure to adhere to ethics has destroyed companies, bankrupted investors, and ruined careers. I am not referring just to ethical wrongdoing at the top of organizations. I also refer to the day-to-day ethical compromises of too many employees at all levels of the organization. In underperforming cultures, especially predatory and political cultures, it is not uncommon for employees to engage in unethical conduct against their coworkers to support their own careers. Too many senior executives claim ignorance or just do not care about the conduct of employees down in the organization. In these companies widespread accountability is seriously lacking.

CREATING A CHANGE-READY CULTURE allows a company to respond more effectively to changing conditions in the marketplace. The very best companies have cultures that actually create change in the marketplace, which gives the company a huge competitive advantage. The oft-quoted statement "Lead, follow, or get out of the way" no longer applies. It is now lead or lose. Too many businesses fail to meet their goals because they are held back by a bureaucratic, frozen, or political cultures. These outdated cultures are self-absorbed and lack an understanding of the marketplace. Change-ready cultures are constantly focused on the marketplace and keep it first in mind.

BUILDING FLEXIBILITY INTO THE CULTURE is critical if a company is to respond swiftly to its competitors. New Age and service cultures allow their companies to respond to marketplace change by minimizing bureaucracy while promoting open communications. They also support independent decision making and action taking around the company. With today's current trend of building ever larger corporations through mergers, companies have more trouble, not less, in responding to change. Newly merged companies need to find ways to reduce the negative effects of a merger. Downsizing alone is not the answer.

ENCOURAGING RISK TAKING AND INNOVATION are hallmarks of high-performing companies and especially those with New Age and service cultures. Breakthrough ideas, critical thinking, and self-initiative need to come from any area of a company without being encumbered by controlling management, a rigid and slow-moving bureaucracy, or an excessively politicized culture. In today's fast-paced environment, companies need to encourage innovation and permit appropriate degrees of risk taking, or they will be passed by their competition. Most companies today are risk averse and do not tolerate mistakes. In those companies, employees keep their good ideas to themselves. It is by learning from our mistakes, not successes, that we make our greatest breakthroughs. Russell Ackoff, professor emeritus at Wharton, noted that risk takers were once the highest paid employees in companies, but no more. Increasingly, the highest rewards are being reserved for the most privileged in companies (*The Democratic Corporation,* Oxford University Press, 1994).

CREATING WIDESPREAD WORKER EMPOWERMENT is essential if a company's management wants to encourage innovation and critical thinking. Unfortunately, most managements tolerate little employee empowerment or autonomous decision making. Bureaucratic and frozen cultures have fostered workforces in which people avoid increased autonomy, even if it is offered to them. Managers will have to demonstrate a greater sense of trust in their employees, and employees in each other, if they want breakthrough ideas, products, and services that will propel them past the competition.

CREATING A DEMOCRATIC WORK ENVIRONMENT must be a primary goal of the culture building process. Too often, democracy seems to stop at the front door of corporations. People are not free to express their ideas and opinions nor to criticize their superiors without risking their jobs. As a result, companies feel emboldened to extend their control over the behaviors and freedoms of their suppliers, customers, and the larger society. We have seen where Wal-mart so closely controls its suppliers that the suppliers have lost the ability to run their business affairs as they see fit. Suppliers that do not strictly comply with Wal-mart demands may suffer mightily in terms of lost business. Economist John Kenneth Galbraith liked to say that "the two greatest threats to democracy are the Kremlin and the American corporation."

CHANGING PEOPLE'S BELIEFS, BEHAVIORS, COMMITMENTS, AND VALUES is a paramount goal for changing a company's culture. Without this change in attitudes and behaviors, the other goals cannot be achieved, and the company has merely put itself through another theoretical exercise.

IDENTIFY ALTERNATIVE QUALITIES FOR THE NEW CULTURE. Companies undertaking the culture change process need to conduct a gap analysis between the prevailing qualities of the current culture and those that are needed to sustain performance. This process requires true courage on the part of the organization, as it implicitly entails rejecting many of the existing qualities and replacing them with new and sometime alien qualities by which the new culture will be known. While each organization needs to tailor those qualities and characteristics to its own unique set of competitive circumstances, the following graphic may provide some guidelines that distinguish between traditional and high-performing cultures.

IT'S ABOUT THE CUSTOMER. The ultimate objective of building and maintaining effective corporate cultures is to satisfy the marketplace—the customer. As Howard Levin, former CEO of Digicon Electronics, kept saying to his employees, "Everything we do is based on serving the customer and the customer will determine how long we remain in business." Companies with strong service cultures build their strategies and cultures around customer needs and expectations.

Figure 8.1 Corporate Culture Qualities

PERFORMANCE-DRIVEN CULTURES	TRADITIONAL AND FAILING CULTURES
CUSTOMER (MARKET) ORIENTATION	PRODUCTS/PROCEDURES ORIENTATION
ASKS "WHY NOT?"	ASKS "WHY?"
ASKS "WHAT CAN WE DO?"	ASKS "HOW CAN WE DO IT?"
LEADERSHIP FOUSED ON ORGANIZATION	LEADERSHIP FOUSED ON STRUCTURE
ATTRACTS AND KEEPS GOOD PEOPLE	RECRUITS AND LOSES PEOPLE
ASKS IF NEW EMPLOYEE CAN BE PRODUCTIVE	ASKS IF NEW EMPLOYEE'S PERSONALITY FITS IN
MISTAKES OF COMMISSION (ASKS FORGIVENESS/LEARNS/MOVES ON)	MISTAKES OF OMISSION (ASKS PERMISSION/DISPLACES BLAME/AVOIDS RESPONSIBILITY)
COURAGEOUS AND PROACTIVE LEADERSHIP	CONTROLLING-INCREMENTAL-REACTIVE LEADERSHIP
OPEN TO RISK TAKING AND NEW IDEAS	RISK AVERSE AND RELIES ON CONVENTIONAL IDEAS
OPEN/NOISY/SELF-EXAMINING	QUIET/CLOSED/SELF-PROMOTING
FOCUSES ON VALUE ADDED	FOCUSES ON PROFITS AND LOSSES (MARGINS)
ENCOURAGES OPEN AND DEMOCRATIC WORK ENVIRONMENT	PROMOTES CLOSED AND AUTHORITARIAN WORK ENVIRONMENT
ANTICIPATES CHANGE	RESISTS CHANGE
ACTS STRATEGICALLY AND DRAMATICALLY	ACTS INCREMENTALLY AND CONVENTIONALLY
FACTS AND RESULTS DOMINATE DECISION MAKING	POLITICS DOMINATES DECISION MAKING

©1995 J. Want, *Managing Radical Change*, Wiley

BARRIERS TO THE CULTURE CHANGE PROCESS

THE WRONG SPONSORSHIP

It is important to identify potential barriers to the culture change process before starting. The change process may cause feelings of alienation and dislocation, especially in those who feel that they are losing authority, turf, or privileges. *Many people are just not comfortable in letting go of the status quo.* According to MIT's Edgar Schein, a company's culture will not change unless certain psychological needs are recognized and satisfied within the organization.

1. *Survival anxiety is high.* People have a high need for membership, competence, and identity. If the change process threatens those needs, people will be reluctant to commit to it. Therefore, the culture change process must replace those old psychological needs with new ones that will provide opportunities for membership, competence, and identity that will match or exceed previous needs.

2. *Learning anxiety is high.* This says that all people are reluctant to lose their skills or be forced to put them aside. People do not like to show their ignorance or be humiliated. The change process must promote people's opportunities to acquire new competencies. It is natural that people will feel threatened by the change process, especially those with the most to lose. This is another justification for having the highest level sponsorship. (E. Schein, *Organizational Culture and Leadership,* Jossey-Bass, 1995)

The culture change process is too important to delegate solely to human resources or another function. Too often, the CEO tells the chief human resource officer to lead the change process (or the chief marketing officer, as at GE), which will doom it to failure. This only trivializes the change process and makes it "another HR project." Neither can CEOs just sign off on the process. They have to establish clear expectations of the organization for the level of commitment that is required and how the change process is to be accomplished. If the CEO and other senior officers are not committed to changing the culture, and are not seen to be fully involved, then no one else within the organization will be committed. The CEO's own high level of commitment will also neutralize pockets of resistance.

"WE HAVE NO TIME: THE COMPANY IS IN TROUBLE"

This is one of the most common excuses for not engaging in the change process. Companies struggling to survive almost always resist dealing with their own failed cultures. The managements of most struggling companies do not recognize that the culture is frequently an underlying contributor to current problems. We saw in chapter 1 that culture is directly linked to bottom-line performance. Too often, companies drift between boom and bust, never recognizing that a performance-driven culture will help the company compensate for many of the down periods that almost all companies encounter. Many problems related to strategy, operations, or customer dissatisfaction and defections find their roots in the culture. The culture building process can also help to uncover hidden strengths of the company. Periods of stress for a company provide the best opportunity for taking a hard look at the culture while starting to change it. Most important, the culture building process provides long-term benefits to the company, especially for dealing with future boom-and-bust cycles. Ignoring the culture of a troubled company can only serve as a detriment to its survival.

"WE HAVE NO NEED: THE COMPANY IS DOING FINE"

Companies that are riding on the wave of success feel no need to tamper with the status quo; examining the culture is the farthest thing from their thoughts. As one company COO said to me, "Let sleeping dogs lie." Nonetheless, current profitability is no predictor of future success or of the culture's readiness to serve the company during difficult times. Again, companies that compete in notoriously cyclical markets need to take stock of their cultures and not be lulled into thinking—falsely—that all is right with their culture. I have always found it interesting that companies that lead their industries are more in touch with how their cultures contribute to sustained success.

BANKRUPTCY

Corporate bankruptcy protection has become a cure-all for failures in the corporate world. Rather than allow companies to fail and fall by the wayside, as intended in an open and free marketplace, our society has allowed bankruptcy to be misused to protect companies against outright failure. We need only look at most of the bankrupt companies in the airline, paper, and steel industries to confirm this. Bankruptcy has also served to shield corporate leaders from the consequences of their own failed leadership and allowed them to avoid dealing with their failed cultures. Delphi, a large auto parts manufacturer that was spun off from General Motors in 1999, filed for Chapter 11 bankruptcy protection in 2005. Like the airlines, Delphi has used bankruptcy protection to shield it, not just from its creditors, but from its own contractual commitments to its employees. When Delphi was spun off from GM, it should have undertaken a thorough appraisal of its culture and begun building one that was more performance-oriented and inclusive of everyone in the company. If it had, it might have avoided bankruptcy.

When a company enters into bankruptcy protection, it sets aside resources to deal with problems of the company as part of its turnaround plan. This prominently includes funding for consultants to advise in the turnaround plan. The usual turnaround plan is centered on downsizing and new marketing initiatives. Companies in this situation should be putting the corporate culture-building process at the top of the turnaround plan. At the least, a company emerging from bankruptcy protection should make culture building a priority.

One bankrupt company that persistently ignored its culture problems was US Airways. Rarely has there been a company in any industry with such serious culture problems as US Air. I am confident of my judgment that it was US Air's culture that forced it into bankruptcy and kept it there. US Air was the carrier of last resort for most fliers, as they knew they would be subjected to poor service and outright abuse by both the workforce and management. Former CEO Steven Wolf never understood the gap between customer expectations and the airline's failure to measure up to those expectations. As a result, it was persistently in and out of bankruptcy. Its merger with America West has done little to correct its deeply ingrained culture problems. Too many companies have utilized bankruptcy as a strategic tool instead of a signal to close down.

EXCLUDING PEOPLE FROM THE CHANGE PROCESS

As I discussed earlier, changing a company's culture cannot be undertaken by excluding people of the organization from the change process. Too many business leaders prefer to hold important corporate initiatives hostage to an elite group of officers and planners, as Jerry Levin did at Time Warner. No change will take place as this need to control is but another addictive behavior. Business organizations are among our most important social organizations and any successful change process must include their people.

ORGANIZATIONAL FRAGMENTATION

Companies with fragmented cultures are in great need of culture building. They have great difficulty in marshaling their resources to be competitive in the marketplace. Key functions within the business are not working together, and there may be open warfare between divisions or senior executives. I have frequently seen where a company's structure may lead to fragmentation preventing the parts of the company from coming together in a holistic business. Very often, fragmentation is seen between management and the workforce (especially where there is a union) or between senior management and the rest of the company.

When a company's leadership grants itself special privileges and exorbitant rewards, while insulating itself from accountability, it has fragmented the culture. Many times senior executives have insulated themselves from accountability and risk. The company may fail, and the CEO may even be fired, but top management leaves with huge golden parachutes. This show of greed only serves to alienate the workforce from management, creating further fragmentation or schisms within the culture. An alienated workforce and middle management cadre will not fully commit to the company or give it its best effort. Culture building can be a major force for bringing a fragmented company back together.

OVERRELIANCE ON FADS, FIX-ITS, AND MAGIC BULLETS

I devoted an entire chapter to the corporate world's obsession with fads and fix-its and their consequences. I will only reiterate here that the magic bullets of restructuring, downsizing, outsourcing, BPR, and a host of operational and productivity enhancements will do nothing to compensate for an underperforming business culture. There are limits to how much productivity can be squeezed out of an organization's operations, and at a certain point, such efforts can only harm a company's culture. In the wake of Merck's serious culture lapses, the new CEO, Richard Clark, should be making a serious effort to improve the company's culture and restore it to its former reputation. Clark's mandate for downsizing and operational fix-its (what Clark knows best from running Merck's manufacturing unit) will not compensate for a failed culture.

INCREMENTAL RESPONSES TO CHANGE

In light of the radical changes confronting companies today, incremental steps for changing the culture will usually fail. Change strategies must be proactive, far-reaching, and quick to take shape. Ambitious goals and forthright action plans need to be put in place to ensure that the culture-building process will be successful. Change comes so rapidly in today's business climate that incremental responses are obsolete before they can be implemented.

Outsourcing and offshoring. Companies in all industries now engage in outsourcing and offshoring for the purpose of displacing overhead, expenses, and possibly gaining greater efficiencies. Some companies also do it to rid themselves of a failed culture. Culture building is especially important when companies start to outsource and offshore operations. Maintaining a common culture in far-flung parts of the country and globe will ensure that a company's ethical standards as well as product and service standards are maintained. A major problem for companies that have outsourced phone call centers to Asia is that the dedication and urgency for serving the customer is greatly diminished through foreign workers. As a result, some companies are returning their call center services to the United States and Canada. Many companies that outsourced manufacturing to Mexico found that the quality of goods manufactured south of the border did not measure up to their standards.

"I Don't Give a Damn About the Culture"

This may be the most prevalent obstacle to any culture-building initiative. I have heard it said openly (and I, at least, applaud candor, even if misguided), and I have seen it communicated through people's lack of action and commitment or passive-aggressive responses. In such cases, those who resist the change process should not be forced to participate in its initial stages. They should be given an opportunity at a later period to become involved. In extreme cases, people may have to be transferred or even separated from the company if they demonstrate a continuing desire to undermine the emerging new culture. There is no benefit from initiating the culture-building process when a CEO or an entire senior management team gives little credence to corporate culture. That does not mean that they will not have to deal with the consequences of their company's failing culture.

REQUIREMENTS FOR CHANGING THE CULTURE

If the company is to undertake a successful culture change process, certain requirements or conditions need to be in place.

Develop a Systematic Change Plan

When companies do undertake to change their cultures, they often fail to lay out a predictable and systematic plan. Many times, they just jump in with some isolated focus groups or a survey with vague notions of what they are doing or how they will do it. The change plan must outline objectives, time lines, necessary people to be included in the process, tactics for overcoming barriers, required resources, necessary leadership requirements, as well as anticipated milestones along the way that will mark progress. The plan should also detail the new qualities and characteristics that are to be made a part of the emerging new culture.

Identifying Change Leaders

Identifying the right change leaders can make or break the change process. Too often, the CEO picks a senior officer or the chief human resource officer. This may be a mistake. Their own normal responsibilities may get in the way, and they may have biases that will steer the process off course. Neither are they necessarily representative of the larger organization. People who are excited by the process and have ideas of their own are good candidates for leadership roles, along with capable up-and-coming middle managers. Nor should we overlook rank-and-file employees; they may have a more realistic view of the culture than anyone in management. When I help a client company identify people who can lead the change process, I look for the squeaky wheels within the organization. The change leader may also be a sage, longtime employee who has a sense of the company's history as well as the recognition that the company needs to change its culture. This type of leader can be an asset in winning over recalcitrant workers and managers.

These culture change leaders should come from all over the organization and have a keen awareness of the implications of the change process for the organization. *The company must commit its very best people to lead the change process.* Most important, they must believe in the change process. The organization needs to know that the change leaders have the full backing and authority of the CEO (and the board, too) and senior management team and that they can go anywhere they want and have the resources they need to be successful. Typically, there need to be several leaders, each to take charge of a key component or objective of the culture building process: communications, decision making, management effectiveness, innovation and risk taking, organizational behaviors, design and structure, and knowledge and competence.

When I conduct a culture audit or organization performance review for a company, I utilize both consensus team building seminars (qualitative) as well as survey instruments (quantitative). Consensus-building sessions provide opportunities for participants to express their ideas, levels of commitment, and leadership skills and are a good forum for identifying potential leaders for the change process. Take notes on who speaks up and what they suggest. These qualitative team-building opportunities also provide insights that no survey instrument can reveal, such as the "whys" and "hows" that will be critical to the assessment and change process.

In addition, there should be an expert or a small team of experts who can advise the leaders. These advisors may be from an internal organization effectiveness department or outside consultants who can provide expert support for purposes of research and process management.

OPENNESS TO NEW IDEAS

Both the change team and the larger organization need to be open to hearing new ideas, no matter how different they may be. A common characteristic of failing cultures is that they are not open to new ideas.

BUILDING A BROAD CONSENSUS FOR CHANGE

Consensus Team Building for Change® is both a concept and a specific intervention process to be utilized with groups of employees within the organization. Consensus building is not just a form of compromise to get people through a meeting, *and it is most definitely not a focus group*. Properly run, consensus-building sessions allow people to share their divergent views and subsequently bring those views together to forge strong consensus beliefs around key culture issues. With proper monitoring and effective process-management skills, consensus-building sessions can be a positive way to build cohesion as well as common commitment. Consensus building also helps to reveal important "constructs" that are not normally discussed openly in the organization. Shortly after the breakup of AT&T, I had the opportunity to lead change management consensus-building teams at NYNEX (forerunner of Verizon) and Contel (an Atlanta-based telecom company). There were stark differences between the two cultures that surveying, alone, did not readily reveal. Prominent were attitudes and commitments between middle-level managers in the two companies. At Contel, there remained a commitment to taking market share away from AT&T and the Baby Bells through innovation and by delivering new products and technology to the marketplace before its competitors. Consensus-building sessions at NYNEX revealed that "making it through to retirement" was a major construct. These two very different middle-management constructs said a lot about the two companies and their cultures.

Construct psychology was pioneered by the psychologist Albert Ellis. Ellis demonstrated that people can look at the same subject or issue while interpreting it differently. In effect, we all have thick lenses in front of our eyes, all focused differently. Within a company, you would expect employees to share a common perspective and opinions about the company. This is not necessarily so. Even if employees share some common overall beliefs, employees within the same company will have divergent beliefs about the company, no matter how subtle. This is especially prevalent in predatory, chaotic, or political cultures. These divergent beliefs can make a major difference in a company's performance and in how people come together to create a common, performance-driven culture. Since the issue of corporate culture usually creates many strong and divergent belief systems, consensus building is a powerful tool in bringing people together to forge a new culture. Everyone's lenses are recalibrated to create a common perspective on the company's culture and what the new culture needs to be. As consensus building grows, people from around the company are attracted to the process. *This becomes a dynamic process of inclusion, and eventually a tipping point is reached where the momentum dramatically shifts to building a new culture.*

ELIMINATE BIAS FROM THE CHANGE PROCESS

Bias is a major obstacle to business performance, but few in the business world recognize the pitfalls of bias. It is only natural for people to overlook their own biases and label them as legitimate, strongly held beliefs. As a result, businesses frequently make critical decisions with long-term consequences based on biased information and belief systems. One of the responsibilities of the leaders of the change process (and their expert advisors) is to be vigilant in watching for bias that may lead the culture building process in the wrong direction. When evaluating the progress of the culture-building effort, objective measurement tools need to be employed that will reduce bias to a minimum. Consensus team building is a powerful tool for identifying and reducing bias amid the culture building process and needs to be implemented by experts who understand the behavior of individuals within the context of a larger organization.

Bias-free quantitative data gathering (i.e., surveying) continues to be an area of need in the business world. Hardly a month goes by when I do not see a poorly constructed survey instrument that clearly has a strong bias, or is improperly constructed, or has misleading wording, all of which can obscure results. I blame both the consulting world and the corporate sector for tolerating this level of incompetence, as it affects the culture-building process as well as other initiatives.

INDIVIDUALIZE CHANGE STRATEGIES

No two business organizations are alike, even if they are competitors in the same industry. An approach that may have been considered appropriate for one organization may not be right for another. Corporations are famous for copying what other companies do, even when what they copy fails to work (see chapter 3). This is another addictive behavior common to the business world. This "lemming" behavior can be attributed to a lack of creativity, a fear of risk taking, or a lack of independent-minded leadership. What is most required for culture building is a strategy that is individualized for that particular company. The process needs to take into account where the company stands in the business-change cycle, external competitive conditions, the age and history of the company, its leadership and management style, its goals for the future, major problems and challenges confronting the company, and, most especially, its current culture.

COMMIT YOUR BEST PEOPLE

The best results can be obtained only when the company commits its best people to the process. The credibility of the process rests largely on the reputations and competencies of the people leading the culture-building process. Every company has its unofficial cadre of "project specialists" who spend most of their careers on special assignments. Over time, they become an internal ad hoc consulting team. These people should not be permitted to take over the culture-building process, for they will have lost touch with the real issues of the day-to-day affairs of the business. They will also have a distorted or unrealistic view of the company's culture. The CEO should pick people from various operating areas of the company covering a variety of disciplines with a few key people from the support side of the business. Ideally, the initial culture audit should be utilized for identifying the people who will serve as the leaders for the culture-building process. When conducting organization audits, I find that consensus-building sessions can be excellent forums for identifying change leaders.

A NEVER-ENDING PROCESS

Culture building is not a onetime "program" with a definitive end point. It does not come to an end to be shelved away in the company's archives. It is an ongoing and evolving process that must keep pace with internal changes in the company and, most especially, external change forces in the marketplace. Too many companies are discouraged from undertaking the culture change process because of this very necessity, despite their never-ending efforts in so many other areas of the company's functioning.

MEASURING THE CULTURE CHANGE PROCESS

Most companies avoid undertaking the culture change process because they do not believe that it can be observed and measured (or they are afraid that they will fail in their efforts to change the culture). Through bias-free processes, progress in the culture change process can be measured both quantitatively and qualitatively. Unfortunately, too few consulting firms and even fewer companies have the ability and know-how to assess their current culture and measure progress in changing the culture. It is just not possible to provide a discourse on the principles and practices of organizational and behavioral measurement within the framework of this book. However, there are certain signs or trends that will show whether the company is succeeding in its efforts to change its culture.

The Culture Is Changing If:

- A dialogue has emerged that questions and even challenges the prevailing culture.
- New behaviors have emerged that run counter to the prevailing or former culture.
- New values and attitudes have emerged that support the new behavior.
- Commitment to the organization for its success and emerging new culture prevails over commitment to the organization for the security it provides.
- New behaviors are pervasive throughout the organization.

- Policies and practices start to change to support new culture norms.
- New competencies begin to emerge in support of daily operations and business practices.

The Culture Is Not Changing If:

- Behaviors and values of the old culture persist under new conditions, crises, or challenges.
- New culture behaviors appear paired with old attitudes, beliefs, and values.
- New culture behaviors are isolated or scattered throughout the organization.
- Former policies and practices that inhibit new culture norms remain in place.
- Former examples of incompetence continue to hold back the organization.

CULTURES VERSUS SUBCULTURES

Large corporations have become hotbeds of many different subcultures. Strategic business units work hard at maintaining their own subcultures, and the reasons often have little to do with performance. The most common reason is to maintain the unit's own distinct identity within the larger corporate parent. This is especially so when a previously independent company has been purchased. People within the business unit take pride in being different and projecting their distinctiveness to both the marketplace and within the larger corporate family. Autonomy is another reason, because business units traditionally resist taking direction from corporate. They want to conduct business their way and frequently believe (sometimes correctly) that corporate headquarters does not understand their needs or even their business. With the trend toward mergers and the rise of multinational conglomerates, this is not surprising, and may even be appropriate when the business unit functions in a different marketplace from the rest of the larger corporation. In many large companies, corporate headquarters is also the source of most administrative support and direction in such areas as human resources, legal, finance, and regulatory affairs. Justifiably or not, the business units perceive these corporate support functions, and the demands that come with their support, as a nuisance (until they need their help) or an intrusion into their own internal affairs.

GE is an example of a multinational conglomerate with very different businesses competing in very different markets. GE Capital would clearly function in a different manner than would the jet engine business, and that business would have different business requirements from its medical imaging business. It is logical that each business would have rather different cultures in support of its different business strategies. The GE corporate entity is actually a holding company for all of its businesses, and some would say that it has a relatively less well defined culture than its individual business units.

The insurance brokerage and risk management company Marsh McLennan also owns several management consulting firms, including Mercer Human Resource Consulting, Mercer Management Consulting, Mercer Oliver Wyman, Mercer Strategy Consulting, and Delta Organizational Consulting. Given the scandal at Marsh McLennan, these companies are putting distance between themselves and the parent company, for good reason. They have a larger problem in that the consulting firms overlap in some areas of consulting while complementing one another in other areas, but they do not go to market together, and they do not draw on each other's expertise, technology, or talent pools. Corporate has asked the disparate firms to start to find common synergies, but the leaders of each firm have generally resisted. This is an example of how adherence to different subcultures can hinder business performance.

Even in companies that operate in one business arena, the line side of the business will have a different subculture from the support side of the business. Companies should not confuse the need for different operational requirements with the need to have a common culture. One of my more challenging clients was a high-tech printing and media company (serving Fortune 100 companies) that was no longer growing. Constant warfare existed between the officers who ran different functions of the business such as finance, research and development, marketing, production, and distribution. None felt that they had to work cooperatively with their counterparts, and that attitude was seen throughout the organization. Each function had its own way of conducting business, and each developed its own subcultures. This prevented each component of the business from coordinating with other parts of the business. Finance, and its CFO, felt that they should dictate how the other functions of the business should operate and tried to manage them by withholding authorization for spending. The other departments also had their own strongly held prerogatives. Sitting on top of these warring cultures was the CEO, who came to the conclusion that the company was no longer an effective competitor in the marketplace because of the constant warfare. He was receiving too much feedback from customers that they felt like they were having to deal with different companies.

In this company the culture change strategy was built on creating a common culture for the entire business, while doing away with the subcultures. The customer was put at the center of the business, and the new culture was committed to providing an integrated approach to meeting customer expectations, from contracting to delivery of the final product. Finance was removed from operating decisions and was given its own, separate forum for dealing with financial and budgeting matters. Marketing and design were integrated into one function that went to market together. This was not just a change in operations, it was a change in people's commitments and behaviors. Some people had to leave the company, including two vice presidents. The company became a customer-centered business with the culture working solely to serve the customer.

The issue of subcultures is also important at the lowest levels of a company, not just at the top, where strategic decisions are made. In the course of conducting a benchmarking study across two business units at Harley-Davidson, I included rank-and-file union members in problem-solving and consensus-building sessions. At one business unit, union members could not be readily distinguished from supervisors and managers. When lunchtime came, all of the participants elected to work through lunch. At another business unit, union members were more easily recognizable by their overalls and heavy work boots. When lunchtime came, the union members stopped working, took out their lunch pails, and retreated to one side of the room, where they took no more and no less time than work rules dictated. (It should be noted that there were far fewer differences than similarities between the two divisions.) In the course of culture building, subcultures need to be understood and respected at every level of an organization. Even the most inconspicuous department or level within an organization can derail the process.

Companies such as Cisco Systems, Nucor, and Johnson & Johnson are large companies with diversified product lines, but each company believes in supporting a strong corporate culture that commits to:

- ethical conduct in the marketplace and within the work environment,
- best professional business practices,
- continual funding of needed research and development,
- workplace equity (employees share in the wealth generated by the company),
- providing workers with the tools they need to get the job done,
- responding proactively to change and, whenever possible, creating change, and
- dedication to serving the customer.

Companies with strong service cultures and New Age cultures share these types of common culture traits.

SETTING PRIORITIES FOR CULTURE CHANGE

Along with the Business Change Cycle, the hierarchy of corporate cultures not only allows us to better understand and identify different types of business cultures, it also helps to prioritize culture change strategies. While the tools and processes for culture building and change may be common for most types of cultures, the priorities may be different according to where a company is on the hierarchy of cultures.

PREDATORY CULTURES

Priorities for culture building in predatory cultures may be more apparent than in other cultures. The company's moral and ethical compass must be corrected before any other goals can be accomplished. Trying to reeducate company leaders who have engaged in unethical and illegal practices is just not practical and sends the wrong message to the organization and the larger marketplace. They have to be replaced. Failure to replace them will only perpetuate the lack of trust in the company by the marketplace. The same should apply to workers and middle managers within the organization who have engaged in similar behavior.

Key leadership positions have to be filled with people who have demonstrated a strong sense of ethical conduct and achieved success in business. Members of the workforce who remain with the company have to recognize past unethical practices without pointing fingers at particular individuals. Then they can identify and build into the culture alternative behaviors and practices that will support best professional practices. *Outside stakeholders, such as suppliers, customers, and investors, ought also to be brought into the culture change process*, a practice I strongly encourage. The company should also consider calling on past employees who may have been frustrated with the company's conduct. They all may have been the victims of past unethical conduct, and they will also be able to provide more objective feedback to the organization and its new leadership.

FROZEN CULTURES

The very nature of the frozen culture—its unresponsiveness to change and denial of reality—makes the culture change process all the more challenging. As with predatory cultures, different leaders may need to be brought into the company, as a top-down approach is required to rebuild the culture. If the leadership team is to remain in place, education and counseling of that team may have to precede culture building within the organization. Employees within frozen cultures look to management for direction and permission given their reluctance to exercise self-initiative and autonomous thinking. It may be possible to find within the company people who have agitated for change and so could become change leaders. Since open communications and autonomous thinking are rare in companies with frozen cultures, leadership must communicate to the organization that people's divergent opinions and ideas are important and will be recognized. *Permission for out-of-the box thinking and self-initiative must be bestowed on the workforce*, and middle and senior management must be open and responsive to these new ideas and risk taking. Any managers who cling to old behaviors that restrict new ideas and initiatives must be separated from the company. In addition, new people from the outside must be brought into the organization for their new ideas, experiences, and talents.

CHAOTIC CULTURES

Chaotic cultures are frequently the product of inexperienced or incompetent management. Leadership and management coaching is one tool to apply with executives and managers to start to change the culture at the top. Many times, they simply do not know how to lead and manage. When a company's management is able to demonstrate more reliable and stable management behavior, the organization will begin to take notice and follow their lead. Management can then develop a mission and strategy that the larger organization can come to rely upon. Setting achievable goals coupled with reliable behaviors and communications is key to transforming a chaotic culture to one that is consistent and reliable.

POLITICAL CULTURES

Political cultures need to be benchmarked against higher performing cultures in order for managers to better understand the gaps that exist between their own culture and that of others. Since political cultures harbor a number of counterproductive addictive behaviors, the reinforcements for those behaviors need to be identified and eliminated. This requires a new system of rewards and recognitions that will support team building, cooperation, and other positive behaviors that support performance. People within political cultures more readily recognize their differences than their commonly shared beliefs and goals. As a result, the culture-building process needs to rely heavily on consensus team building to identify shared goals and business objectives. Consensus building will also identify people who can work together and want to work together in coalitions.

BUREAUCRATIC CULTURES

Businesses with bureaucratic cultures have lost track of the customer. Their own internal requirements, rules, policies, and practices take precedence over customer needs. As a result, the customers' needs must be put at the center of the culture change process. I strongly recommend that customers also be included in the culture change process. Many bureaucratic companies blame regulatory requirements for their inability to shed their bureaucratic cultures. In such cases I urge companies to segregate their bureaucratic functions from those areas that are directly involved in serving the needs of clients and customers. Identify the bureaucratic or regulatory requirements they cannot shed and put a firewall up between them and the areas of the business that serve the customers. For this to be successful, a new set of behaviors must be identified and encouraged that will replace bureaucratic behaviors. These are to be based on placing the needs of customers before the bureaucratic requirements of the organization.

SERVICE CULTURES

Service cultures have a totally opposite objective from bureaucratic cultures. They must not lose track of those qualities and characteristics that have made them strong service cultures. A major threat to service cultures is the tendency to become too "operationalized." Overreliance on policies and rigid operational requirements reduces the culture's ability to individualize for customers. Airlines and utilities are examples of companies that have become so dependent upon fixed operational measures that they lose the ability to address special needs or unforeseen customer problems. The customer is no longer at the center of the service model.

NEW AGE CULTURES

New Age cultures face twin challenges: chaos and too much success. Chaos is the order of the day at Google. Its founders have shown a unique ability in technological innovation, but little in leading and building a cohesive organization. Their chosen CEO, Eric Schmidt, demonstrated little talent for organizational leadership at Novell. With the continued fast growth of the company, chaos may keep it from taking advantage of future opportunities or will blind it to new initiatives from such rivals as Microsoft or future "Googles" that do not yet exist. Much of the chaos can be attributed to their rapid success as well as their unwillingness to deal with the critical organizational issue of corporate culture. Managing success can be as difficult as managing failure, for many successful companies become predatory. Microsoft is an example of a company with a former New Age culture that has become a predatory culture. This "opportunity" to become predatory is a major threat to companies with New Age cultures.

CULTURE BUILDING FOR SMALLER COMPANIES

I frequently hear leaders and managers from smaller companies say that culture building is for large companies. Nothing could be farther from the truth. As the leaders (and many times founders) of smaller companies and their workforces struggle with day-to-day operational issues, they feel that culture building must be put off into the future while they deal with the "important issues" of running the company. Cultures of smaller companies are more easily managed and redirected than larger companies, and it is less costly to deal with the culture issues of a smaller company.

Leaders of small companies may put off attending to the company's culture, but the culture begins to emerge on its own at once; it will not wait for executive directives or guidance. Just as other aspects of a company's functioning, such as operations, human resources, marketing, finance, and quality improvement, do require directed leadership and day-to-day management, it is too convenient to put off issues related to the culture. *Unfortunately, a company's culture takes on a life of its own and waits for no one to manage it. In smaller companies, the culture grows as rapidly as the business.* If ignored, the culture can go off in the wrong direction just as quickly, and jeopardize the long-term survival of the company.

I was invited to make a presentation on culture to the executive team of an IT software consulting firm. It had experienced tremendous growth in its first five years as it served the software needs of midmarket and major government contractors. Overnight it grew from the original founders and a handful of employees to several hundred employees located in several cities. By all accounts, the company was successful, but problems were starting to arise that were beyond the understanding and usual operational interventions of the owners. Of paramount concern was that necessary communications and direction were just not getting out to employees. New plans and practices were not being implemented. Common standards for best professional practices did not exist. Commitments made by the owners to clients were not being fulfilled. At one point, they had to halt critical hiring as they could not ensure the proper training of new hires, much less their integration into the company.

As the company grew, expanded to other locations, and ramped up with new personnel, the culture evolved on its own and got out of control. The owners and senior managers admitted that they gave no attention to the company's culture and felt that directives from headquarters were enough to ensure that the company "ran as we wanted it to run." One field office seemed to have a "culture of its own." People brought a lot of "their own baggage with them from their former employers." Policies and practices were selectively enforced by location or by the client project. What troubled the owners most was that cliques were arising around strong or charismatic personalities who were building "boutiques" within the company. The owners and several of the senior managers realized that the culture was taking charge of the company, and they acknowledged that they needed to take charge of it. The owners finally dedicated themselves and the company to building the culture around a well-defined set of qualities and goals that the owners believed were necessary to sustain the business. They also recognized that their long-term plans for the company would never be realized until they dealt with the culture.

9

CHOOSING TO CHANGE THE CULTURE

We need more stewardship and less salesmanship.

—John Bogle, Founder, Vanguard Funds

Change has become the primary influence on how companies conduct business and plan for the future. A few outstanding companies systematically incorporate change into their planning and business operations, and they rely heavily on their corporate cultures to support performance. Most companies, however, are simply driven by the forces of change. Change has become the overwhelming force that drives business to success as well as to failure. While the business world has been a major source of change for modern society, companies slavishly cling to old and outdated business cultures that hinder performance and prevent them from adapting to change. No company can hope to steer its way through a radically changing competitive environment without understanding its own culture and developing the means to manage it in support of its strategic goals. *Just as production processes, marketing plans, and workforce capabilities need to be constantly adjusted to changing market conditions, so must a company's culture.*

Savvy investors know that markets are driven by psychology, and so, too, companies. "They are first and foremost human organizations" (A. Gabor, *The Capitalist Philosophers,* Harvard Business School Press, 1999). A company's culture is a reflection of that human organization. *To ignore how a company functions as a social system of human beliefs, aspirations, capabilities, and performance is to ignore the very nature of the business organization itself.* That is why downsizing, business process reengineering, operations improvement, restructuring, and outdated business planning have so consistently failed to improve the performance and functioning of business organizations. They actually damage their cultures because they ignore the human element.

Gordon Bethune, former CEO of Continental Airlines, succeeded Frank Lorenzo and had the enormous task of rebuilding the company. Bethune immediately recognized that the culture had to be rebuilt if the company was to survive. Bethune liked to say that "whatever problems you run into in running a business, they are all people problems. Businesses are run by people. At the root of whatever problems you have in a business you'll find people. A lot of managers and executives miss the forest for the trees by forgetting to look at the people" (Scott Huler, *From Worst to First,* Wiley, 1998).

When Arie DeGeus was director of planning for Shell Oil Company, he conducted a study to determine how long Shell might expect to remain in business. He determined that the typical successful company had an average life expectancy of forty to fifty years. He also found that a full third of all Fortune 500 companies existing in 1970 no longer existed in 1987 (A. DeGeus, *The Living Company,* Harvard Business School Press, 1997). That means that such industry-leading companies as Microsoft, Cisco Systems, and Intel may already be halfway through their life cycles. What does that imply for less successful companies and for the larger American business community? The Shell study found that the longest surviving companies exhibited four key traits, three of which were related to culture:

1. They were sensitive to their external environment.

2. They were socially cohesive, with a strong sense of "community and identity." They fostered feelings of belonging to a social system or culture. While not guaranteeing lifelong employment, long-term employee tenure is often the rule. At the same time, internal learning and organizational regeneration processes minimize complacency within the culture.

3. The companies are tolerant, even supportive, of internal change processes. This means that they tolerate initiatives that are taken on the margins of the company by people who may have eccentric ideas and notions.

4. They are financially conservative. They focus on preserving capital.

3M is a company that fits this profile. In its deliberate, process-oriented manner, 3M has been the harbinger of many major and minor product breakthroughs over decades of its existence. It is a company that innovates but in many small ways and without a lot of fanfare. It does not set out just to make new products; it invents new processes and practices that are widely emulated throughout the business world. It has also found a way to encompass a multidisciplinary culture of professionals that allows people on the fringes of the business as well as those at its core to engage in the discovery and development of products. As a result, 3M may have one of the most enduring New Age cultures in the business world as it continues to develop—not just grow.

Under its new CEO, Paul Otellini, Intel is undertaking a major change process. The strategy ranges from changing its famous logo and slogan—"Intel Inside"—to undertaking a major diversification of its product lines and a move away from its traditional engineering-centered R&D to one that includes multidisciplinary teams. Many people within the company, and some customers, are already alienated by Otellini's plan (but former CEOs Andy Grove and Craig Barrett endorsed the initiative), and turnover at the company has reached 4 percent, which exceeds high-tech industry averages. This may be a reflection of natural selection: People who opt out of the change process would probably resist or even sabotage it. The company's long-term success will depend heavily on whether it decides to put culture change at the core of its business and technology change effort. Otellini's courageous decision to undertake a new strategy for the company must be matched by an equally courageous leadership in changing the Intel culture.

SETTING PRIORITIES

According to David Wickenden, senior vice president of Fleischman-Hillard, an international marketing and public relations firm, companies spend many millions of dollars on branding. SBC spent tens of millions of dollars on changing its name to AT&T, and Intel will spend at least $1 million in consulting fees alone to change its logo and marketing slogan. It will spend several million more to replace its famous logo and slogan on products and marketing tools. Verizon spent more than $5 million to put its name on the indoor sports coliseum in Washington, D.C. (formerly the MCI Center). By comparison, the money spent on culture building by companies is minuscule. Would companies do better if they spent a portion of that money on building ethical, performance-driven business cultures?

THE CULTURE BUILDING PROCESS IS UNIQUE

Changing a company's culture is unlike any other corporate intervention. The critical difference is that *changing a company's culture is about development and not just growth*. It is a *qualitative* process that addresses such issues as leadership capabilities, efficacy of a company's mission, identity, management effectiveness, commitments, values, behaviors, cohesive and cooperative workforces, innovation, team building, competencies, openness and trust, performance and accountability, communications and decision making. These issues drive the more familiar functions of a business, such as operations, distribution, R&D, business strategy, marketing, and information technology. Too often, companies put all of their energies and resources into these more familiar aspects of the business without looking at the culture, when it is the culture that affects all aspects of a business.

Changing a company's culture involves the entire organization—not just one function, management layer, or division. A company's culture is a reflection of many *stakeholder* interests that go beyond the usual *shareholders* of the business. To be effective and credible, *culture building must be a holistic process that encompasses every aspect of the business and all of its stakeholders*. When a company excludes a key stakeholder constituency from the culture change process, it alienates a key component of its ecosystem. A company is a reflection of many interests and contributions that extend beyond investors: employees, who contribute their thinking, talents, personal efforts, and careers; suppliers and contractors, who provide outside resources and knowledge; and customers, who provide the very justification for the existence of the business. Many business interventions can be accomplished within a discrete portion of the business or through a single constituency, but culture change requires a holistic approach to be successful.

Experienced change leaders understand that *courageous and farsighted leadership* is required if the culture change process is to succeed. Sensitivity to politics is important, but those who engage in perpetual political compromise are not the right leaders for the culture change process. Best professional practices, no matter how unpopular, must have their champions or the culture change process will collapse under the weight of discord and divisive politics. The cultures of most companies have a natural bias to control or put down ad hoc leaders. Natural leaders who champion innovative ideas are almost always threatening to an organization. John Kenneth Galbraith referred to this phenomenon as the corporate pursuit of the "culture of contentment" (J. K. Galbraith, *The Culture of Contentment*, Houghton Mifflin, 1992). *If a company is to change its culture, it must experience a good deal of discomfort with the old culture*. This is one reason why courageous leadership and sponsorship is required. It provides direction, protection, and legitimacy for the appointed change leaders as they systematically enlist support for changing the culture. That, in turn, attracts new recruits to the emerging new culture from around the organization.

Changing a company's culture is not just about a company's immediate needs and challenges. It must have a *future orientation*. High-performing and effective cultures are not static but are continually evolving. Companies that take their cultures seriously provide systematic and ongoing direction and support. They look to the future to determine the kind of culture they will need. Unfortunately, most corporate cultures today are static, rigid, and resistant to change. Corporate leaders reinforce this unchanging nature of the culture by mistakenly believing that stasis is a positive attribute of the company's culture. Continuous change will dictate that business cultures continue to evolve and change to keep pace or the company will lose its competitiveness.

Changing a company's culture is about *risk taking*. It asks people to think and behave in different ways and to replace old and outdated commitments and values with new ones that will enhance their own performance as well as that of the larger organization. Companies with high-performing cultures support risk taking and allow a certain amount of failure. Companies with static cultures rarely recognize missed opportunities and creative new ideas that could move the company forward. They also fail to recognize innovative talent within their own walls.

The culture change process must also inspire the company to reach for a higher set of goals and principles for *ethical behavior*. Green Mountain Coffee Roasters has been cited by *Business Ethics Magazine* as number one on its list of ethical companies, but that has not prevented Green Mountain from registering record profits. People's widely shared principles for moral and ethical conduct should not be discarded when they report to work. Too frequently, that seems to be the case. A company's conduct and values should be consistent with the values of the larger society.

THE FORK IN THE ROAD

The American corporation is poised at a critical juncture. It may continue to enable obsolete business cultures that restrain performance (and force unethical conduct to obscure that failed performance), or it can transform its centuries-old culture into an entirely new type of dynamic business organization. *In recent years, trends in the business world have been directed toward making more money at any cost, which has undermined human performance and the desire to work. As a result, too many of today's business cultures are dominated by:*

- fear,
- poor morale,
- incompetence,
- mediocre products,
- aversion to risk,
- bad customer relations,
- unhealthy behaviors and work relationships,
- poor quality,
- unethical conduct,
- reduced innovation,
- uninformed management,
- authoritarian work environments,
- transitory commitments,
- fragmented, underperforming organizations, and
- inconsistent financial performance.

This culture will only produce companies with short life spans that fail to satisfy the expectations and needs of investors, customers, or workers. It will only serve to continue the current trend that has turned the business world into a lottery.

The alternative is to build companies that have effective, high-performing cultures that are characterized by:

- trust,
- strong morale,
- widespread worker and organizational competence,
- products that are in great demand,
- openness to reasonable risk taking and experimentation,

- effective and mutually beneficial customer relations,
- productive behaviors and positive work environments,
- products and services of consistent high quality,
- unswerving ethical conduct,
- well-informed and thoughtful management,
- consistently high levels of innovation,
- democratic work environments,
- long-term commitments between all stakeholders,
- unified, high-performing organizations, and
- consistently strong financial performance.

Companies that build and maintain cultures with these qualities are vastly better equipped to outlive the expected life span of the typical company and will be better able to take advantage of the radical change that continually roils business markets. Since corporations—of all sizes—play an increasingly dominant role in modern society, the stakes are too high for American business and the United States economy to not invest in our corporate cultures. For survival and effectiveness in the new business world, it is all about change.